To Isabel Myers and Mary McCaulley
who taught me about type theory,
and to my family—Cherie, Karen, and Mark—
who showed me how it works.

CONTENTS

Chapter Three: Developmental Needs And Type Concepts

INTRODUCTION

Lisa is a problem for her teachers. She's bright enough, but she seems to value popularity above everything else. Talkative, friendly and gregarious, she relies on her friends to make decisions for her and she patterns her behavior after theirs. Adults see her as flighty, unsure of her own preferences and point of view. Her work and conversations are often trite and shallow. Sometimes her classmates are annoyed by her "helpfulness;" they wish she would mind her own business. When criticized by a teacher or her friends, she seems deeply hurt and resentful.

Lisa frustrates her teachers; this is not because she disrupts class or resists assignments. The problem is that they realize her personal development is not going well and they feel powerless to do anything about it. Perhaps, through their planning meetings, they can focus on a strategy to help Lisa develop some perspective and "a mind of her own." But at least 50 more of the students they see every day need attention as much as Lisa does. There is not the time to work out a strategy for each of them.

Matching instruction to each student's uniqueness is, in most situations, an unrealizable objective. Yet to ignore individual differences in learners is foolish. Without straining to attend to uniqueness, it is possible to identify patterns in students that can serve as shortcuts to matching instruction to individuals. Consider Lisa's case, for example. Do you see in her a pattern you recognize? Probably every classroom has a "Lisa." The teacher who can recognize the basic ingredients in Lisa's behavior, who can see a motivation pattern, can then make an educated, shortcut prediction about what teaching strategy will work best with Lisa.

This book presents one way to identify learning styles and motivation patterns and it shows how to use the patterns in planning instruction. Behind the book lies a long, personal search by the author to find practical and effective means of matching instruction to basic differences in students. A variety of approaches exists. Many of them merit attention. The approach presented here is based on Carl Jung's ideas about psychological types, as made practical through the work of Isabel Briggs Myers.* Theirs is a remarkable theory that offers a fresh perspective on people's patterns of dealing with their world.

This book includes readings and instructions for activities that explain the theory and guide you in making applications of it. The book may be used to guide a workshop or as a basis for group study; or it may be used by individuals. The activities that are designed for small groups can be accomplished by individuals with the occasional assistance of a colleague. The book is addressed specifically to teachers, but many other people in the helping professions should be able to translate the ideas and activities to their professional framework.

INTRODUCTION TO THE SECOND EDITION

Responses to the first edition were very encouraging and made this new edition possible. Readers helped me see the need for additional material. Chapter One now contains an expanded introduction to Jung's theory of types. It also includes a new section giving answers to questions often asked about type. Robert Duch has written a chapter on introducing type theory into a school system.

As my own understanding of type has deepened, I have needed to make small changes throughout the book to give the presentation more clarity and precision. Special thanks go to Alan Brownsword and Mary McCaulley for careful and enlightening critiques that stimulated many improvements in the wording.

Since the first edition appeared, a new membership organization for people interested in type has been formed—the Association for Psychological Type. It is described at the end of the book in the section entitled Next Steps in Using Type Concepts.

---

*Jung, Carl G. *Psychological Types*, Princeton: Princeton University Press, 1971 (Original edition 1921). Myers, Isabel Briggs. *Gifts Differing*. Palo Alto, California: Consulting Psychologists Press. 1980.

People Types and Tiger Stripes

1

People's habits tell a lot about them. Not just their "bad habits," but also such habits as what they pay attention to, what they care about, and how they decide things. These are mental habits.

Do you know any people with mental habits like these? Chris is quick to notice people's feelings, and tries to stay out of arguments. Jan likes to argue, likes to explain things, and doesn't notice people's feelings. John's father wants him to keep a careful record of how he spends his weekly allowance. John says record keeping isn't important to him. Pat wishes her mother would watch the clock more and get to places on time. Pat's mother wishes Pat would relax and not get an ulcer over being late five minutes.

Some mental habits are very deep in a person. Trying to change them is like trying to change the stripes on a tiger—like trying to change the grain in a piece of wood. The information that follows is about mental habits—the kind we probably can't change but can learn to use better.

PATTERNS OF MENTAL HABITS

The deep mental habits come in patterns, in combinations. Described below are eight patterns you can use to study yourself, your friends and family. Pick out your own patterns. There are no right or wrong patterns. Think carefully and try to pick the patterns that really describe you best. This exercise is not a test. It is simply a way for you to start looking at the patterns in yourself.

After you have completed the exercise, you will be able to see how the eight sets form into patterns of people types, and you can get an idea of which type may be yours.

Exercise: Thinking about Mental Habits

Which pattern describes you better, E or I?

E	I
E *likes action and variety*	**I** *likes quiet and time to consider things.*
E *likes to do mental work by talking to people*	**I** *likes to do mental work privately before talking*
E *acts quickly, sometimes without much reflection*	**I** *may be slow to try something without understanding it first*
E *likes to see how other people do a job, and to see results*	**I** *likes to understand the idea of a job and to work alone or with just a few people*
E *wants to know what other people expect of him or her*	**I** *wants to set his or her own standards*

E's interest turns mostly outward to the world of action, people and things. I's interest turns more often to the inner world of ideas and private things. Everyone turns outward to act and inward to reflect. You must do both, but you are more comfortable doing one or the other, just as right-handers are more comfortable with the right hand. **E I** Circle the E or the I in the margin to show which pattern fits you better.

> E stands for extraversion, which means outward turning.
> I stands for introversion, which means inward turning.

Which pattern describes you better, S or N?

S	N
S *pays most attention to experience as it is*	**N** *pays most attention to the meanings of facts and how they fit together*
S *likes to use eyes and ears and other senses to find out what's happening*	**N** *likes to use imagination to come up with new ways to do things, new possibilities*
S *dislikes new problems unless there are standard ways to solve them*	**N** *likes solving new problems, and dislikes doing the same thing over*

S *enjoys using skills already learned more than learning new ones*	**N** *likes using new skills more than practicing old ones*
S *is patient with details but impatient when the details get complicated*	**N** *is impatient with details but doesn't mind complicated situations*

S pays most attention to the facts that come from personal experience. S can more easily see the details, while N can more easily see the "big picture." N pays most attention to meanings behind the facts.

S and N are two kinds of perception, that is, two ways of finding out or giving attention to experiences. S stands for sensing and N stands for intuition. Everybody uses both their sensing and their intuition to find out things. You use both, but you use one more than the other. Circle **S N** the S or the N in the margin to show which pattern fits you better.

Which pattern describes you better, T or F?

T	**F**
T *likes to decide things logically*	**F** *likes to decide things with personal feelings and human values, even if they aren't logical*
T *wants to be treated with justice and fair play*	**F** *likes praise, and likes to please people, even in unimportant things*
T *may neglect and hurt other people's feelings without knowing it*	**F** *is aware of other people's feelings*
T *gives more attention to ideas or things than to human relationships*	**F** *can predict how others will feel*
T *doesn't need harmony*	**F** *gets upset by arguments and conflicts; values harmony*

T makes decisions by examining data, staying impersonal and cool. T stands for thinking judgment. F makes decisions by paying attention to personal values and feelings. F stands for feeling judgment. You make T and F judgments every day, but you use one kind of judgment more **T F** than the other. Circle the T or F in the margin to show which pattern fits you better.

3

Which pattern describes you better, J or P?

J	P
J likes to have a plan, to have things settled and decided ahead	**P** likes to stay flexible and avoid fixed plans
J tries to make things come out the way they "ought to be"	**P** deals easily with unplanned and unexpected happenings
J likes to finish one project before starting another	**P** likes to start many projects but may have trouble finishing them all
J usually has mind made up	**P** usually is looking for new information
J may decide things too quickly	**P** may decide things too slowly
J wants to be right	**P** wants to miss nothing
J lives by standards and schedules that are not easily changed	**P** lives by making changes to deal with problems as they come along

J P Circle the **J** or **P** in the margin to show which pattern fits you better. **J** stands for judgment and **P** stands for perception. **J** people show to others their thinking or feeling judgment more easily than they show their sensing and intuitive perception. The opposite is true for **P** people; they show their sensing or intuition rather than judgment in dealing with the world outside themselves.

Types Come From Patterns

Now you can put together the four letters of the patterns that describe you best. Draw a circle here around the same letters you circled in the margins above.

E I S N T F J P

Now write your four letters here: _____ _____ _____ _____
The four letters together make up a whole pattern called a "type." It may be your type.

There are 16 different "people types" as shown by the 16 combinations of the letters. Find yours.

ISTJ	ISFJ	INFJ	INTJ
ISTP	ISFP	INFP	INTP
ESTP	ESFP	ENFP	ENTP
ESTJ	ESFJ	ENFJ	ENTJ

4

Each type is different from the others in important ways. As you come to understand the type ideas better, you will see how type affects your life with your friends and family, at school or in a job.

The activity you have just completed is one you may want to use with students. With young students in mind, I wrote it in as simple language as I could. You may photocopy and reproduce the activity for students, giving credit to this publication. Use it only as a discussion starter, as a first step in thinking about type. It is not an instrument developed by research.

Why Types and Patterns are Important

This book shows how an understanding of type is important to teachers and other professionals concerned with instruction and guidance. In my own work to understand student motivation and learning style, I have come to the conclusion that type is fundamental. It is crucial in explaining why certain instruction works with some students and not with others. The fact that a student prefers sensing perception over intuitive perception, or prefers an active (extraverted) approach to studies over a reflective (introverted) one, is not just an interesting curiosity. It is information that some teachers have used to make dramatic improvements in the effectiveness of their instruction.

The Myers-Briggs Type Indicator

The four dimensions of type (EI, SN, TF, and JP) and the ideas behind the sixteen types represent the lifelong work of Isabel Briggs Myers. In 1962 Educational Testing Service published the Myers-Briggs Type Indicator, a paper and pencil instrument she developed with Katherine Briggs over a twenty year period. Regarded as a research instrument, it did not have wide circulation or usage until Consulting Psychologists Press assumed responsibility for publishing it in 1975. The Indicator was developed specifically to carry Carl Jung's theory of type (Jung, 1923) into practical applications.

The rest of this book will be more useful to you if you have taken the Indicator and are aware of your own profile. The Indicator was written to be taken by people who have not yet studied about type. Spontaneous responses probably give a more accurate profile, so the time to take the Indicator is before you proceed with this book. If you have not yet taken it, inquire about a local source that can administer it and give you information about your type. Persons qualified to order instruments from Consulting Psychologists Press may order the Indicator from them. The address is: 577 College Avenue, Palo Alto, California 94306. Write for a price list. The question booklets are reusable. There are two means of scoring the responses: by handscoring keys that can be purchased from CPP, or by a computer scoring service that provides each person with a print-out of his/her type profile and an interpretation of it. To obtain a price list and order form for computer scoring write: Center for Applications of Psychological Type, Inc., P.O. Box 13807, Gainesville, Florida 32604.

CPP and CAPT also distribute *Introduction to Type* by Isabel Myers, a booklet that gives a basic explanation of type concepts. Because *Introduction to Type* is a necessary resource for interpreting your results from the Indicator, it has been reproduced in this book as an Appendix.

If your responses to the Indicator are scored by the computer service, your print-out will show your profile and a description of your type. If your response sheet is handscored, look up the description of your four-letter type in *Introduction to Type* (the Table of Contents on page A-1 will show you where to find your type description).

Look again at the type formula you chose while reading "People Types and Tiger Stripes" activity. If it does not agree with the type derived from the Indicator, look it up in *Introduction to Type* and compare the two descriptions. Decide which one best matches you. Keep in mind that the Indicator is a carefully researched instrument and the "People Types" exercise is not. Don't expect to understand type concepts quickly. Their meanings will present themselves to you at times and in circumstances that will surprise you. For now, read *Introduction to Type*, all 18 pages, with special attention to pages A2-A6.

JUNG'S THEORY OF PSYCHOLOGICAL TYPES

The great Swiss physician-psychologist, C. G. Jung, developed one of the most comprehensive of current theories to explain human personality. Where other observers saw people's behavior as random, Jung saw patterns. What he called "psychological types" are patterns in the way people prefer to perceive and make judgments. In Jung's theory, all conscious mental activity can be classified into four mental processes — two perception processes (sensing and intuition) and two judgment processes (thinking and feeling). What comes into consciousness, moment by moment, comes either through the senses or through intuition. To remain in consciousness, perceptions must be used. They are used — sorted, weighed, analyzed, evaluated — by the judgment processes, thinking and feeling.

The Mental Processes

Perceptive processes: Sensing and intuition *

Sensing (S) is the term used for perception of the observable by way of the senses. **Intuition (N)** is the term used for perception of meanings, relationships and possibilities by way of insight. Sensing (S) types use sensing and intuition, but prefer, and therefore develop, sensing. With good type development, the expertise in sensing can lead to a differentiated awareness of present experience, acute powers of observation, a memory for facts and detail, and a capacity for realism, for seeing the world as it is. Attitudes characteristically developed as a consequence of a preference for sensing include a reliance on experience rather than theory, a trust of the conventional and customary way of doing things, a preference for beginning with what is known and real, and then moving systematically, step by step, tying each new fact to past experience and testing it for its relevance in practical use. To most sensing types, "real intelligence" is characterized as soundness, accuracy and common sense.

Sensing types are attracted to careers and settings where skillful application of well-learned knowledge is more important than developing new solutions; where working with tangibles is more important than using theory and insight; and where dealing with the immediate situation and using conventional wisdom is more important than making bold new breakthroughs.

Intuitive (N) types use sensing and intuition, but prefer and therefore develop intuition. With good type development, intuition provides insight into complexity, an ability to see abstract, symbolic and theoretical relationships, and a capacity to see future possibilities, often creative ones.

Attitudes characteristically developed as a result of a preference for intuition include a reliance on inspiration rather than on past experience, an interest in the new and untried, and a preference for learning new materials through an intuitive grasp of meanings and relationships. To most intuitive types, "real intelligence" is shown by insight in grasping complexities, and flashes of imagination or creativity.

---

*These brief descriptions of the processes of perception and judgment are taken from: M.H. McCaulley. *Applications of the Myers-Briggs Type Indicator to Medicine and Other Health Professions.* HRA Contract 231-76-0051, DHEW, January 1978. Available from Center for Applications of Psychological Type, Inc., P.O. Box 13807, Gainesville, FL 32604.

Intuitive types are attracted to careers and settings where it is more important to find the pattern in complex systems than it is to deal with the practical details; where creating new knowledge is more important than applying existing knowledge, where working with theory and imagination is more important than dealing with tangibles, and where intellectual challenge is more important than the enjoyment of the pleasures of everyday events.

Judgment processes: Thinking and feeling

Thinking (T) is the term used to define a logical decision-rnaking process, aimed at an impersonal finding. **Feeling (F)** is a term for a process of appreciation, making judgments in terms of a system of subjective, personal values. Both thinking and feeling are considered rational processes because they use reasoning to arrive at conclusions or decisions.

Thinking types (T) use both thinking and feeling but prefer to use thinking for making judgments. With good type development, expertise in thinking leads to powers of analysis and an ability to weigh facts objectively including consequences, unintended as well as intended. Attitudes typically developed from a preference for thinking include objectivity, impartiality, a sense of fairness and justice, and skill in applying logical analysis. Thinking types are attracted to areas where tough-mindedness and technical skills are needed.

Feeling types (F) use thinking and feeling but prefer to reach judgments through feeling. With good type development, feeling leads to development of values and standards, and a knowledge of what matters most to themselves and other people. Attitudes typically resulting from a preference for feeling include an understanding of people and wish to affiliate with them, a desire for harmony, and a capacity for warmth, empathy and compassion. Feeling types are attracted to areas where understanding and communication with people is needed, and find the interpersonal skills more interesting than the technical skills.

Dynamic Relationships of the Mental Processes

The dominant process

Everyone regularly uses all four mental processes — sensing, intuition, thinking, and feeling — but we do not use them equally well. From childhood, each of us has come to rely on one more than the others. It seems more trustworthy, and so it is used more and becomes more mature and reliable. That one mental process becomes the centerpost, the core of the personality. People in whom **sensing perception** is the centerpost, the dominant mental process, are above all else practical people. Their close attention to data provided by the senses makes them well attuned to immediate experiences, the literal facts at hand, the concrete realities.

People who have **intuitive perception** as a dominant process are naturally less tuned to sensory experience. Their consciousness is mainly filled with associations, abstractions, theories and imagined possibilities that do not depend directly on the senses. Above all else, they believe in intuitive insights and imagination to set life's directions.

People in whom **thinking judgment** is the strongest mental process are above all else logical, and have orderly, analytical minds. All experience must fit into logical mental systems, or the systems must be reworked to accommodate perceptions that don't fit. Children of this pattern may not seem logical by adult standards, but internally the drive is to test and organize all experience by logical criteria, even if the logic is still undeveloped. They naturally treat people and things (and themselves) objectively.

Finally, people with **feeling judgment** as the dominant mental process direct their lives toward human values and harmony, above all else. They weigh all experience as being harmonious or dissonant with the values and priorities of their own lives and the others they care about. They are naturally more attuned to the subjective world of feelings and values, and more alert to the humane issues in any situation.

The concepts of polarity and balance

In Jung's theory, the two kinds of perception — sensing and intuition — are polar opposites of each other. Similarly, thinking judgment and feeling judgment are polar opposites. In a person with intuition dominant, it follows that sensing is necessarily the least developed and least trusted (and trustworthy) of the four mental processes. That is not an arbitrary feature of the theory, but rather a logical condition in human experience. In the instant that conscious attention is focused on intuitions, it cannot simultaneously be focused on sensations, and vice versa. I may shift quickly from one to the other, but not attend to both at once. Thus, I attend to my intuitive perception and develop my intuitive capacities at the expense of my sensing perception.

If people trusted and developed only one of the four mental processes their lives would be essentially one-dimensional. Unfortunately, we all know such people whose perceptions are not focused or tempered by good judgment. And we know others whose judgments are locked so tightly that they remain unrenewed by fresh perception.

The auxiliary process

To avoid a one-dimensional personality, a person must develop a helping or auxiliary process to balance the dominant process. Because of the polarity concepts just described, the auxiliary is always formed in the dimension that the dominant is *not* in. That is, a person having sensing or intuition as the dominant process will develop either thinking or feeling as the auxiliary process. Similarly, a person with thinking or feeling as the dominant process will have sensing or intuition as the auxiliary process. Thus, combining dominant and auxiliary processes, eight sets are formed:

Dominant		Auxiliary	Dominant		Auxiliary
Sensing	with	Thinking	Intuition	with	Thinking
Sensing	with	Feeling	Intuition	with	Feeling
Thinking	with	Sensing	Thinking	with	Intuition
Feeling	with	Sensing	Feeling	with	Intuition

The meaning of the eight sets can be illustrated by the varied emphases in the left-hand column above. The sensing-with-thinking people focus their practical outlook on the aspects of the world that are readily subject to logical analysis—the objects, machinery, and more impersonal transactions of life. In contrast, the sensing with feeling people attend primarily to the practical side of human needs. Still different in emphasis, the thinking-with-sensing people are those who wish to put their system of logical order on the practical matters of the world. And the feeling-with-sensing people are concerned primarily with harmonious relationships and seek to attain them through practical helpfulness.

The differences suggested here are subtle but not superficial. The intuition-with-thinking people, for example, may test their intuitive inspirations with logical analysis, and the analysis may shoot down the inspiration. However, if the inspiration is compelling enough, no amount of illogic discovered in the idea will be enough to kill it. In a showdown, intuition will win because it is the dominant process in intuition-with-thinking people. In contrast, the thinking-with-intuition person would sacrifice the intuition in such a showdown.

The third dimension

Jung identified a third dimension of personality structure that expands the eight sets to sixteen, and these sixteen are referred to as the Jungian preference types. The third dimension is extraversion-introversion. Jung invented these terms. He created them from the Latin components, and assigned to them quite specific meanings. These meanings have been distorted, if not corrupted, in American common usage. Staying close to the Latin, extraversion means outward-turning and introversion means inward-turning. We all do both regularly, every day. We turn outside of ourselves to act in the world, and we turn into ourselves to reflect. Of course, action is blind and may be fruitless without reflection; and reflection that does not lead to action is futile. However, each person is not equally "at home" in action and reflection. Extraverts often say "When in doubt, act." Introverts are more likely to say "When in doubt, reflect on the matter more deeply."

How does extraversion-introversion fit into the eight patterns already described? People who use their dominant process primarily to run their actions in the world are extraverted. People who reserve the dominant process primarily for the personal world of inner thoughts and reflections are introverted. The dominant process is the best introduction to a person; it tells the most about that person's personality. Extraverts, by definition, reveal their best first. What you see is what you get. Introverts, reserving their best for their inner, their favored world, reveal mainly their auxiliary process to others. Only close associates will be allowed to see the most valued process in operation. Thus we come to know introverts more slowly.

Consider, for example, how the extraversion-introversion dimension expands the thinking-with-intuition pattern. The extraverted version describes those people who want to act in the world and to manage as much of it as they can. They want to extend their personal logical systems into the world around them, which is their favored arena for personal expression. In contrast, introverted thinkers want to exercise their dominant process (thinking) mainly in the inner realm of private mental activity, and they strive above all else to have orderly, logical minds. They use their auxiliary process (intuition), mainly to run their outer (extraverted) lives, and this gives the *appearance* of having intuition as the dominant process.

Simple symbols can show these ideas. Capital letters are used to represent the dominant process and small letters are used to represent the auxiliary process. A circle is used to represent the dividing line between the inner and outer worlds that people live in. Here are two examples:

F Feeling judgment is dominant and extraverted. Sensing
(s) perception is auxiliary and introverted.

s Feeling judgment is dominant and introverted. Sensing
(F) perception is auxiliary and extraverted.

The people represented by the first symbol make their feelings public, naturally and frequently. Their antennae are out to pick up

11

feeling signals, and they are the practical harmonizers and weavers of compromises.

The people represented by the second symbol have no less wealth of feeling, but it is reserved as a private process, and is revealed only to family and close friends. they take a receptive, quiet-helper role, in contrast to the activist and often warmly-aggressive stance of those who have feeling dominant and extraverted.

The fourth dimension

Briggs and Myers elaborated Jung's ideas of psychological type and explicated a fourth dimension that is present, but not highlighted in the descriptions already given. The fourth dimension is the attitude taken toward the outer world. When a judgment process is used in running one's outer life[1], the natural drive is to have things decided, judged, settled, planned, organized, and managed according to plan. This is the judging attitude toward the outer world. In this personality pattern, the drive is always toward closure, toward having a settled system in place.

When a perception process is used to run one's outer life[2], the natural drive is toward keeping things open to new perceptions. The person wants to stay flexible, so as to adapt to changing circumstances, and to experience life as widely as possible. This is the perceiving attitude toward the world. In this personality pattern, the drive is always toward keeping plans and organization to a necessary minimum so one can respond to new perceptions and adapt flexibly to new circumstances.

To summarize briefly, in Jung's theory of psychological types, all conscious mental activity occurs in two perception processes (sensing and intuition) and two judgment processes (thinking and feeling). Everyone uses all four processes, but we differ in how much and how well we use each of them. In every person, one of the processes is dominant and that process indicates the basic way the person addresses life. If a person uses the dominant process mainly in the world of people and things, that person's orientation is called extraverted. The person who uses the dominant process mainly in the inner, private world of ideas and thoughts is called introverted. Balance in personality is achieved by the development of a second of the four mental processes, so that both a perception and a judgment process can be used reliably.

1. As in (S) and (S)   2. As in (F) and (t)

The sixteen types

The MBTI has four scales corresponding to the four dimensions of type theory, as shown in the figure.

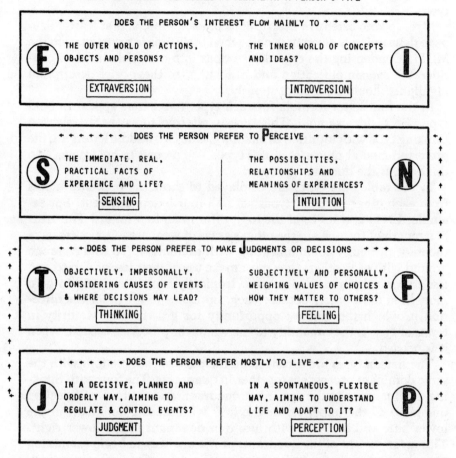

FOUR PREFERENCES ARE SCORED TO ARRIVE AT A PERSON'S TYPE

+ + + + + DOES THE PERSON'S INTEREST FLOW MAINLY TO + + + + + + +

E THE OUTER WORLD OF ACTIONS, OBJECTS AND PERSONS?

THE INNER WORLD OF CONCEPTS AND IDEAS? **I**

EXTRAVERSION   INTROVERSION

+ + + + + + DOES THE PERSON PREFER TO PERCEIVE + + + + + + + +

S THE IMMEDIATE, REAL, PRACTICAL FACTS OF EXPERIENCE AND LIFE?

THE POSSIBILITIES, RELATIONSHIPS AND MEANINGS OF EXPERIENCES? **N**

SENSING   INTUITION

+ + + DOES THE PERSON PREFER TO MAKE JUDGMENTS OR DECISIONS + + +

T OBJECTIVELY, IMPERSONALLY, CONSIDERING CAUSES OF EVENTS & WHERE DECISIONS MAY LEAD?

SUBJECTIVELY AND PERSONALLY, WEIGHING VALUES OF CHOICES & HOW THEY MATTER TO OTHERS? **F**

THINKING   FEELING

+ + + + + + DOES THE PERSON PREFER MOSTLY TO LIVE + + + + + + + +

J IN A DECISIVE, PLANNED AND ORDERLY WAY, AIMING TO REGULATE & CONTROL EVENTS?

IN A SPONTANEOUS, FLEXIBLE WAY, AIMING TO UNDERSTAND LIFE AND ADAPT TO IT? **P**

JUDGMENT   PERCEPTION

The MBTI uses a shorthand designation for the eight characteristics: **E** for extraversion, **I** for introversion, etc. as in the figure. Note that **N** is used for intuition because **I** has already been used for introversion.

While type is reported and explained in four parts, it is not merely a combination of parts. Nor is it static, as the term "type" often connotes. Type is a dynamic system, and each type is an integrated pattern. The accompanying page of brief descriptions of the sixteen types highlights the strengths of each type, and the similarities and differences of the types.

Myers wrote extensive descriptions of each type, and at least a one-page description is given to people when their type is reported from the MBTI. Condensing the type descriptions into one table involves considerable oversimplification and distortion, so these brief description highlights should be used cautiously.

In the four letter formula for each type, two letters appear in bold type, **ENTJ** for example. This type is referred to as the extraverted thinking type with intuition as auxiliary. The two middle letters are the preferred mental processes of this type. The process in bold type, **T** in this case, is the dominant process.

In the table, the types are displayed to show the opposites across from each other — that is, types with all four letters different. For example, **ENTJ** and **ISFP**, at the top, differ in all four letters. The areas of strength of the one are the other's areas of weakness. Opposites have the most difficulty communicating with each other. To find common ground with each other, they must make use of their less preferred and less trustworthy mental processes. Ironically, opposites stand to gain most from each other, because each represents to the other the direction in which the greatest opportunity for growth lies. Maturity in terms of type is the capability to use whatever process is needed, when it is needed.

The sixteen types are arranged on the page so that the four with the same dominant process are together in quadrants. The four with thinking dominant are in the upper left quadrant, and the four with feeling dominant in the upper right; the four with sensing dominant in the lower left, and the four with intuition dominant in the lower right. This arrangement of the quadrants provides a way to begin examining the relationships between learning style and Jungian preference type.

Dynamics of type and the learning process

In my judgment, the most essential relationship between type and learning style can be seen in the nature of the dominant mental process in each personality. Refer again to the brief descriptions of the sixteen types and consider the differences represented by the quadrants, beginning with the types with thinking dominant. The young thinkers

14

Brief Descriptions of the Sixteen Types

E N T J

Intuitive, innovative ORGANIZER; aggressive, analytic, systematic; more tuned to new ideas and possibilities than to people's feelings.

E S T J

Fact-minded, practical ORGANIZER; aggressive, analytic, systematic; more interested in getting the job done than in people's feelings.

I N T P

Inquisitive ANALYZER; reflective, independent, curious; more interested in organizing ideas than situations or people.

I S T P

Practical ANALYZER; values exactness; more interested in organizing data than situations or people; reflective, a cool and curious observer of life.

E S T P

REALISTIC ADAPTER in the world of material things; good natured, tolerant, easy going; oriented to practical, first hand experience; highly observant of details of things.

E S F P

REALISTIC ADAPTER in human relationships; friendly and easy with people, highly observant of their feelings and needs; oriented to practical, first hand experience.

I S T J

Analytical MANAGER OF FACTS AND DETAILS; dependable, decisive, painstaking and systematic; concerned with systems and organization; stable and conservative.

I S F J

Sympathetic MANAGER OF FACTS AND DETAILS; concerned with peoples' welfare; dependable, painstaking and systematic; stable and conservative.

I S F P

Observant, loyal HELPER; reflective, realistic, empathic; patient with details, gentle and retiring; shuns disagreements; enjoys the moment.

I N F P

Imaginative, independent HELPER; reflective, inquisitive, empathic, loyal to ideals; more interested in possibilities than practicalities.

E S F J

Practical HARMONIZER and worker-with-people; sociable, orderly, opinioned; conscientious, realistic and well tuned to the here and now.

E N F J

Imaginative HARMONIZER and worker-with-people; sociable, expressive, orderly, opinioned, conscientious; curious about new ideas and possibilities.

I N F J

People-oriented INNOVATOR of ideas; serious, quietly forceful and persevering; concerned with the common good, with helping others develop.

I N T J

Logical, critical, decisive INNOVATOR of ideas; serious, intent, highly independent, concerned with organization, determined and often stubborn.

E N F P

Warmly enthusiastic PLANNER OF CHANGE; imaginative, individualistic; pursues inspiration with impulsive energy; seeks to understand and inspire others.

E N T P

Inventive, analytical PLANNER OF CHANGE; enthusiastic and independent; pursues inspiration with impulsive energy; seeks to understand and inspire others.

in school are energized by logically organized material; they thrive on things that can be analyzed, and resent anything that must be "learned" which does not fit logically into their mental systems. They respond best to a teacher who is well organized, but they resist and resent the teacher whose organization is not logical. If they do not find logical orderliness in either the material or the teacher, there is no way for them to bring their best energies and effort to the learning tasks.

The types with feeling dominant are in the upper right quadrant of the table. As the young feeling types start a new school year, they test the situation with two paramount criteria: Does the teacher care about me? Is the subject matter something I can give my heart to? If a caring relationship is formed with the teacher, it can carry the young feeling types through many school tasks that don't interest them. But when attachments to the teacher *and* school subjects are both achieved, these children produce at their best. With both conditions absent, they lose their primary motivation, and any adjustments in instructional procedures and physical conditions are likely to make little difference.

Young sensing types, represented in the lower left quadrant, may appreciate logical order and harmonious working relationships, but their learning motivation does not depend primarily on either. Above all else, they respond to what they see as practical and functional. Their criteria are: Can this teacher and this material show me something useful? Will I learn some skills that my senses can master and put to good use? These are the students most likely to become lost when the teacher skips steps in explanations and directions, leaves large gaps for students' imagination to close, teaches abstractions without checking to see whether they connect with concrete realities in the students' lives, and teaches "facts" and "skills" that can only be put to use at some indeterminate time in the future. These are the students who do their best mental work when their senses are fully engaged ("I think best with my hands...").

The last group, the intuition dominant students, are in the lower right quadrant. These students crave inspiration above all else. They are fully engaged only when their imaginations are fired with intriguing ideas and plans. For them, routines quickly become dull. Unless the teacher or the material inspires them, boredom sets in and drives them to seek out something – anything– to relieve the boredom and to reestablish the inspirational spark. Often they resort to daydreaming, to reading off-task material, or to undermining the teacher. Their energy flows wherever inspiration is. When inspired, they are the most innovative of all types.

If teachers were to learn just one thing about psychological types,

16

the thing most important to understand is the power of the dominant process. If the best learning is to happen, thinking types must pursue logical order; feeling types must follow their hearts; sensing types must strive to engage their senses in the mastery of practical skills; and intuitive types must follow whatever inspires. To capture the interest of diverse students requires real artistry in teaching. Understanding the power of the dominant mental process makes that task a little easier.

The inferior process

For each type, it is also important to remember which mental process is the least used and least trusted. That process is always the polar opposite of the dominant process, as sensing is the oppostie of intuition, and as thinking is the opposite of feeling. Jung called the opposite of the dominant process the "inferior" process. Some others refer to it as the "shadow." (Jung used the term shadow to cover more than the inferior process.) The inferior process is the least developed and most childish of the processes when it does appear. It is the process we have the least control of, and is the one that has taken over when we say "I wasn't being myself just then."

In Gifts Differing, Isabel Myers argues for helping the inferior process to develop by letting it play, but not by pressing it into service. When working with a sensing dominant student, for example, the teacher is not helping, and is probably harming, the student by requiring learning activities that depend mainly on intuition for a sustained time. And with intuition dominant students, the surest way to bring out their worst behavior is to keep them on tasks that require them to follow uninspiring routines, step by step, with careful attention to details. The inferior process can be developed in two ways, according to Myers. First, the inferior process can be developed by letting it play — giving it outlets that are recreational, such as when intuitives enjoy hobbies like woodworking. Second, the inferior process can be developed by letting it serve the dominant process in some way that is very important to the dominant. An illustration of this second method can be found in the work of Isabel Myers herself. She was an INFP, an introvert with dominant feeling, and her heart's desire was the perfection of the Type Indicator. To accomplish this goal, prompted by her dominant feeling, she mastered statistics and research design, and would spend weeks of mathematical work to discover one fact that might improve the Indicator.

Being aware of the dominant and inferior mental process is especially important when working with students whose types are most different from one's own. The teacher who effectively engages students' attention and interest does so by finding some common mental ground. In type theory, the common ground includes shared perceptual data and/or shared value judgments. These usually are easy to anticipate in students who are like us in type, but they are hard to find in students whose types are unlike our own. Fortunately, the study of type gives us ways to understand and work with the mental patterns of different types, even when we can't "be there" and know existentially what they are experiencing.

Questions Often Asked About Type

How does a person get to be a type?

By doing well what comes naturally. One of the four mental processes (S, N, T, or F) and one attitude (E or I) are your natural bent, according to Jung, and these natural preferences make up the heart of type. He believed that we are born with a dispositon for one type. Environmental factors are very important, since they can foster type development, or get in its way. Type may not be clear in young people; that is, the dominant process may not yet be differentiated enough to organize and integrate the personality. The first task of a young person in type development is to differentiate the dominant process. A later task is to gain balance by developing the auxiliary process. The other two processes have to be developed, at least passably, because all four processes are needed every day of our lives. In middle life, some few people keep on developing, and may become more expert with the third, and even the inferior process.

How do you know if a mental process is developed or differentiated?

Jung said you could tell because it would be "strong, stable, consistent, reliable, and adapted to the situation." When we are not yet differentiated in type, we may be able to recognize our lack of development because we don't feel self-sufficient.

How do you develop a mental process?

By using it purposefully to achieve something you think is important. A good example comes from the use of sensing. Development of sensing gives a sense of reality and excellent powers of observation. If you are sitting on a train, watching the scenery go by, you are using your sensing but not particularly developing it. If you are driving yourself around a strange city, you will probably concentrate your sensing to notice and remember landmarks — this process develops your sensing.

Doesn't type fence you in?

Not if you understand it. An understanding of type frees you in several ways. It gives you confidence in your own direction of

18

development — the areas in which you can become excellent with most ease and pleasure. It can also reduce the guilt many people feel at not being able to do everything in life equally well.

As Isabel Myers puts it, "For most people, really understanding their own type in particular, and other people's types in general, is a releasing experience rather than a restricting one. It sets one free to recognize one's own natural bent and to trust one's own potential for growth and excellence, with no obligation to copy anyone else, however admirable that person may be in his or her own different way."

Can you change your type?

Scores in the Myers-Briggs Type Indicator can be changed depending on how you answer the questions. Score changes can result in a *report* of a different type. Jung seemed to believe that each person has a true type that he or she may not yet have discovered. The true type does not change, although it may seem to, as one focuses on developing different mental processes at different stages of one's life.

However, there are many reasons you might take the MBTI two different times and come out different types. You might still be discovering your preferences, and trying them on for size. Or you might be working especially hard to develop one of the mental processes, so that you report it on the MBTI with stronger than usual emphasis. Or, you might take the MBTI one time as your "job self," responding as you see yourself acting on the job, and you might take it another time as your "home self," responding as you see yourself in your home environment. If your type differs in two reports, this fact may lead to interesting information about yourself, as you cast your mind back to your frame of mind when you were answering the questions.

How do you discover your true type?

Start with what you are sure about. Read all the descriptions with the preferences you are sure of. At this point, you may find a type that you know is yours. If you are still puzzled, start observing yourself. For example, if you are undecided about thinking or feeling, start noticing how you make decisions. Are decisions better if you trust your heart (**F**) or your head (**T**)? Notice when activities take a lot of energy and effort. See if you can identify which mental process you were using. It is often true that preferred processes seem effortless, and less preferred processes are more tiring. For example, if watching details closely for a long time makes you feel tired, cross, or nervous, you might investigate whether other sensing activities are also hard for you. You could then look to see if intuitive activities come more easily. If they do, you could consider whether intuition might be your preferred process. To test

19

these ideas, you could ask yourself if your hunches, flashes of inspiration and other intuitions are generally accurate or trustworthy.

What is the best type to be?

For you, the type you really are.

Is everyone of the same type alike?

No. There are many individual differences within each type. Some people are more differentiated, or at a higher level of type development than others. Even in well-developed types, there are big differences. Take an ESFJ for example. You would expect all the ESFJ's to share a wish for people around them to be happy, and would work to achieve harmony. Some ESFJ's might be interested in education and be teachers; others might become family doctors and others salespersons. Still others might find their way of helping in volunteer work, or in being a good parent. All these activities would give ways of using feeling in the outer world, as extraverted feeling types are predicted to do.

Do some types make better teachers than others?

All sixteen types are represented among teachers who have answered the MBTI. Each type has its characteristic strengths and limitations. Each makes special contributions to teaching. Students come in all sixteen types. At times, all students need the support of being with a teacher who is like them in type, because understanding comes more easily between similar types. At times, every student needs the challenge of being with a teacher of a different type. Finding the right balance between support and challenge for students is an important task for those who plan instruction. If a faculty has a mixture of types, and knows about the characteristic strengths of different types, then students can be better served.

What types commonly become teachers?

To understand the proportions of the different types among teachers, it is first useful to know the distributions of the types in the general population. The best estimate is that in the general population, extraverts outnumber introverts in a proportion of two or three to one; sensing types outnumber intuitive types in approximately the same ratio. Women come out about 60% feeling types, and men come out about 60% thinking types. In the general population, judging types outnumber perceptives with about 55% J and 45% P.

The table shows the proportions of teachers holding MBTI preferences at various teaching levels. These data came from the data bank which is a product of the scoring services of the Center for Applications of Psychological Type in Gainesville, Florida. The table shows occupations recorded by teachers from around the country whose MBTI answer sheets were sent in for scoring. One group of 5363 teachers simply described themselves as teachers.

Extraverts and introverts are about equally represented at all levels of teaching. The proportion of intuitive types increases as grade level rises. Feeling types are in the majority through high school, with thinking types outnumbering feeling types in college teachers. At all levels judging types outnumber perceptive types. Administrators tend to have even more judging types than do teachers.

Type Preferences of Teachers

Teacher Group	Number	EI	SN	TF	JP
Teachers (unspecified)	5363	52 % E	52 % S	63 % F	63 % J
Elementary	517	52 % E	61 % S	69 % F	66 % J
Middle and Junior High	940	53 % E	54 % S	82 % F	64 % J
High School	426	51 % E	51 % S	59 % F	67 % J
Junior College	484	52 % E	60 % N	55 % T	61 % J
College and University	1378	52 % I	65 % N	50 % T	63 % J
School Administrators	904	59 % E	53 % S	51 % F	70 % J
College Administrators	203	53 % E	61 % N	51 % T	68 % J

TALK ABOUT TYPE CONCEPTS

I have explained the Myers-Briggs Type Indicator and type concepts to many teachers. Nearly all of them have benefited from talking about the concepts with colleagues, family, and friends. You are likely to get the most out of this book if you are part of a group of four or five colleagues using the book together. This is a good point to begin your discussions, if you have not started talking already. Convene a meeting. Each person should bring to the meeting: MBTI profile and this book. In addition the group will need several apples, at least one for each person. Here are some suggestions for the agenda of your meeting. Keep your own notes for possible further use.

Exercise: Discussing Type Concepts

A . Share your reactions to your MBTI profiles. If you know each other well, you may want to guess each other's type formula.

B . The object of this meeting is to help each other understand the concepts of "people types." Raise questions you have about the concepts. Your group may want to review specific portions of *Introduction to Type.*

C . Discuss opposites, dominants, auxiliaries and shadows, using the "Brief Descriptions of the Sixteen Types."

Exercise: Eat an Apple*

Now you can stop wondering what the apples are for. They are to help you get a deeper insight into the four mental processes — sensing, intuition, thinking and feeling. Follow these activity instructions:

A . This activity is to help you distinguish the mental processes of perception (intuiting and sensing) and judgment (thinking and feeling). Work in pairs with one partner being a recorder. The recorder should mark off four sections on a sheet of note paper. Label one section Sensing, one Intuition, one Feeling, and one Thinking. As both partners talk, the recorder should make notes in each section, as indicated below, starting with sensing. Each person selects and eats an apple, paying attention to each of the four processes separately, one at a time. Take three or four minutes for each process.

1) As you eat the apple, list your sense impressions of the apple and its parts: skin, flesh, carpels, seeds — noting colors, shapes, textures, tastes, muscular movements and tensions. List facts only.

2) List your intuitions that come to you during the experience. Memories and associations: Who or what do apples make you think of? Can you recall other ways of enjoying apples? baked? jellies or ciders? games? other? Do you recall apples in stories, myths, poems, proverbs, or superstitions? Do you find yourself speculating about this particular apple?

3) Can you think about apples?
Did your sense impressions or your intuitions lead you to make any logical conclusions about this apple? About apples in general? "I'd say this apple has been in cold storage. I say that because..."

4) List your feeling judgments:
How you felt about trying this experiment.
How you felt about selecting the particular apple you did.
How you felt about eating the apple you chose.

*The idea for this activity was suggested by Alan Bundick.

22

B . Each recorder read to the others in the group what was written in the sensing section. Get concurrence that all items were sensory data. Then read each of the other three similarly.

C . The group then discusses this question: In what ways is the set of data recorded under "sensing" fundamentally different from the kinds of things listed under "intuition?" Do all members of the group agree? Do the two sets of data help to show why people who perceive with their senses more than with their intuition, and who dwell more on sensory data than intuitive data, are fundamentally different from intuitive types (and vice versa)? Can you see why they would be more tuned to concrete facts, in the "here and now," and less tuned in to abstractions, imaginings, possibilities and speculations? Now consider the notes under "feeling" and "thinking." How are these two kinds of judgment statements basically different? Do they help to show the real differences between **F** types and **T** types?

CHECK YOUR KNOWLEDGE OF TYPE CONCEPTS

Before going on to applications of type to educational settings, you may wish to see how well you grasp the concepts. Here is a word list you can use to review the ideas. Following that is a Type Concepts Test and answer key with which you may check your responses. After you are reasonably sure you understand type concepts, the following activities will make a practical check of your understanding.

First, you might find several people (colleagues, family, students, etc.) who are interested in taking the Myers-Briggs Type Indicator. Arrange to have them take it, explain the theory to them, and, if appropriate, have them check their comprehension with the Type Concepts Test. (This activity is less cumbersome than it sounds.) Typically, people who learn about the MBTI want to talk with someone about it. This activity encourages you to talk about type concepts with care, and thereby will test your comprehension of the theory.

Second, you can select a professional colleague to be a partner. Select a colleague whose type is different from yours. Arrange to observe each other informally in several different situations. Then, discuss with each other the ways that type shows up in everyday behavior. You will want to use the booklet *Introduction to Type* for ideas of what to observe, and as a resource in developing your capacities to observe each other.

23

Words to Help Understanding of Type Concepts

Sensing Perception: When using my sensing I am...

Perceiving with the five senses
Attending to practical and factual details
In touch with the physical realities
Attending to the present moment
Confining attention to what is said and done
Seeing "little things" in everyday life
Attending to step-by-step experience
Letting "the eyes tell the mind"

Intuitive Perception: When using my intuition I am...

Perceiving with memory and associations
Seeing patterns and meanings
Seeing possibilities
Projecting possibilities for the future
Imagining; "reading between the lines"
Looking for the big picture
Having hunches; "ideas out of nowhere"
Letting "the mind tell the eyes"

Thinking Judgment: When reasoning with thinking, I am...

Using logical analysis
Using objective and impersonal criteria
Drawing cause and effect relationships
Being firm-minded
Prizing logical order
Being skeptical

Feeling Judgment; When reasoning with feeling, I am...

Applying personal priorities
Weighing human values and motives, my own and others
Appreciating
Valuing warmth in relationships
Prizing harmony
Trusting

Extraversion: When extraverting, I am...
Oriented to the outer world
Focusing on people and things
Active
Using trial and error with confidence
Scanning the environment for stimulation

Introversion: When introverting, I am...
Oriented to the inner world
Focusing on ideas, concepts, inner impressions
Reflective
Considering deeply before acting
Probing inwardly for stimulation

Judgment: When I take a judging attitude, I am...
Using thinking or feeling judgment outwardly
Deciding and planning
Organizing and scheduling
Controlling and regulating
Goal oriented
Wanting closure, even when data are incomplete

Perception: When I take a perceiving attitude, I am...
Using sensing or intuitive perception outwardly
Taking in information
Adapting and changing
Curious and interested
Open-minded
Resisting closure to obtain more data

Dominant Process
Favorite among S, N, T or F
Governing force
Unifies one's life
Best developed and most used process
"The ship's captain"

Auxiliary Process

Second favorite among S, N, T or F
A perceptive (S or N) process if the dominant is
judgment (T or F)
A judging (T or F) process if the dominant is
perception (S or N)
Used in the outer world if the dominant is introverted
Used in the inner world if the dominant is extraverted
"The ship's first mate"

Inferior Process (Sometimes called the shadow)

The opposite of the dominant (as S is opposite N,
T is opposite F)
The least developed process
Our relatively childish and primitive perception or judgment
An escape from the conscious personality
Is in charge when "You don't act yourself"
A source of much undiscovered personal energy

Type Concepts Test*

Record your multiple-choice responses on a separate sheet and check your answers with the key which immediately follows the test. Some of the items have more than one correct answer.

1. Type theory is concerned with the valuable differences in personality that result from
   a. basic mental health
   b. environmental influences
   c. the way people perceive and judge
2. The term "dominant process" in type theory means
   a. either extraversion or introversion
   b. either a judging or perceptive attitude
   c. the favorite process, the one used most
3. The auxiliary process is
   a. the opposite of the dominant
   b. the least used process
   c. the second favorite
4. If the favorite process is a judging one, the second favorite is
   a. also a judging one
   b. a perceptive one
   c. any of the other processes
5. If the second favorite process is a judging one, the favorite will be
   a. a perceptive one
   b. also a judging one
   c. any of the other processes
6. By extravert is meant
   a. a gregarious type who talks a lot
   b. a shallow person
   c. one who prefers to focus on people and things
7. By introvert is meant
   a. one who prefers to focus on ideas and concepts
   b. one who is aloof and unsociable
   c. a neurotic

---

*This test was originally developed by Anna Nuernberger.

8. By sensing type is meant
   a. one who is sensitive and empathic
   b. one who is sensuous
   c. one who prefers to perceive through the five senses
9. By intuitive is meant
   a. one who has prophetic powers
   b. one who values imagination, inspirations and possibilities
   c. one who has extrasensory perception
10. By thinking judgment is meant making judgments
    a. by means of all the mental processes
    b. logically and impersonally
    c. taking into account all the data
11. By feeling judgment is meant
    a. immature, emotional judgments
    b. irrational and illogical judgments
    c. judging on the basis of human motives and values
12. One's orientation to life is either
    a. judgment or perception
    b. extraversion or introversion
    c. the dominant or the auxiliary process
13. One's attitude toward the outer world is
    a. either judging or perceptive
    b. governed by the favorite process
    c. governed by the second favorite process
14. The effects of the combinations of perception and judgment
    a. are arbitrary and unpredictable
    b. produce the different types of personalities
    c. produce different sets of interests, values, needs, habits of mind and surface traits
15. Sensing plus thinking people are mainly interested in
    a. facts, which can be collected and verified by senses and analysis
    b. possibilities which reveal themselves in new data and experiences
    c. problems which allow them to use their ingenuity
16. Sensing plus feeling people are mainly interested in
    a. the impersonal and logical handling of other people
    b. making decisions about facts which take into account how people feel
    c. problems which allow them to use their imagination

17. The intuition plus feeling people are most interested in
    a. projects that involve them with equipment and tools
    b. possibilities for people
    c. facts about projects
18. The intuition plus thinking people
    a. enjoy practical problems
    b. are interested in possibilities which they approach with impersonal analysis
    c. choose projects which do not require executive or technical ability
19. The last letter in the type formula indicates the mental process you use in the outer world
    a. if you are an extravert
    b. if you are an introvert
    c. for both extraverts and introverts
20. The introverts rely on their auxiliary process
    a. for dealing with the outer world
    b. for dealing with the inner world of ideas
    c. in the same way as the extraverts
21. The introverted judging types (with a J in their type formula) have as their favorite process
    a. a judging process, either thinking or feeling
    b. a perceptive process, either intuition or sensing
    c. any of the four mental processes named above
22. The extraverted judging types (with a J in their type formula) have as their favorite process
    a. a judging process, either thinking or feeling
    b. a perceptive process, either sensing or intuition
    c. any of the four mental processes named above
23. The well-developed auxiliary process is necessary
    a. to prevent superficiality in the introvert
    b. to help the extraverts put their best foot forward
    c. to help both extravert and introvert achieve balance, and keep them from ignoring either world
24. In types whose favorite process is a judging one, the perceptive auxiliary provides
    a. help in making quick decisions
    b. the raw material needed as a basis for judgment
    c. a second line of attack when the favorite process does not work

25. In types whose favorite process is a perceiving one, the judging auxiliary provides
    a. a steadiness of purpose
    b. a means of evaluating the worth of their perceptions and the uses to be made of them
    c. help in suspending judgment when data are insufficient
26. The remaining processes, after taking into account the dominant and auxiliary
    a. should be suppressed
    b. are not necessary, and can be ignored
    c. can make contributions toward greater effectiveness
27. A high score (over 20) on a dimension of the MBTI means
    a. a well-developed process
    b. a definite preference
    c. neglect of the opposite process
28. A low score (under 10) on a dimension of the MBTI means
    a. a less well-developed process
    b. little preference between the choices
    c. that both processes may be developed almost equally well
29. The "tendencies" of the types
    a. are the way people are and nothing can be done about it
    b. are the talents you can aspire to realize, and the warnings of what to guard against
    c. are among the most useful learnings you can experience from understanding type theory
30. Certain types
    a. will have trouble with other types
    b. can be of more use to you than other types
    c. will be easier to understand than other types
31. In conflicts, you can use your understanding of type
    a. by being sensitive to the other person's type
    b. by being certain that the other person is aware of your point of view
    c. to understand what it is that one of you sees and values more highly than the other
32. In education, you can use your understanding of type
    a. to plan more effective learning situations according to type
    b. by expecting a person to focus on processes intrinsically comfortable to him
    c. to plan situations which exercise all the processes and give children broad choices in developing their own type preferences

30

Answers to the Type Concepts Test

1. c. the way people perceive and judge. (Sensing and intuition are the perceiving processes; thinking and feeling are the judgment processes.)
    a. *Basic mental health is assumed to be associated with good type development, but it is not the basis of the theory.*
    b. *Environmental influences can indeed affect the way types develop. but they are not the main concern of type theory.*
2. c. the favorite process, the one used most. (Sensing, intuition, thinking and feeling are mental processes, one of which will be the favorite or dominant.)
    a. *Extraversion and introversion are defined as attitudes, not mental processes.*
    b. *A judging or perceptive attitude describes how one runs one's outer life, but does not reveal the dominant process.*
3. c. the second favorite
    a. *The opposite of the dominant conflicts with it and therefore is the least developed of the four processes. The auxiliary, to be helpful, must serve the dominant process, not compete with it.*
    b. *The opposite of the dominant is the least used, least trusted process.*
4. b. a perceptive one. (It's responsibility is to supply facts and understanding as a basis for judgment.)
    a. *If both dominant and auxiliary were judging processes, there would be no balance. Also, the auxiliary would be opposite the dominant.*
    c. *The opposite of the dominant is excluded as a candidate for the auxiliary*
5. a. a perceptive one. (When the second favorite process or auxiliary is a judging process, it is because the favorite or dominant process is perceptive and needs a judging assistant for balance.)
    b. *If both dominant and auxiliary were judging processes, there would be no balancing perception.*
    c. *One of the other processes would be the inferior function, which cannot be the favorite.*

31

6. c. one who prefers to focus on people and things

   a. and b. answers may reveal prejudices you need to look at. Introverts may see extraverts as over-talkative and shallow, because introverts have little way of knowing how satisfying the company of others can be to extraverts.

7. a. one who prefers to focus on ideas and concepts

   b. and c. choices may indicate, either that you do not understand the meaning of the word "introvert", or that you have a prejudice which can affect your dealings with introverts. If you are an introvert yourself, you may lack the allegiance to your own type which is necessary for an effective and happy personality.

8. c. one who prefers to perceive through the five senses

   a. and b. are not correct. Being a sensing type brings with it no assurance that one will be sensitive, empathic, or sensuous.

9. b. one who values imagination, inspiration and possibilities.

   a. and c. are not correct. Having a preference for intuition over sensing is no assurance that one has, or can attain, prophetic powers or extrasensory perception.

10. b. logically and impersonally

    a. In general language, "thinking" is often used to describe all the mental processes. In type theory, "thinking" is restricted to judgments made in a logical, impersonal way.

    c. Sensing perception is more associated with seeing all the data.

11. c. judging in the basis of human motives and values. (A feeling judgment is one that comes to a rational conclusion by weighing the different human values and motives involved.)

    a. and b. are not correct. Emotion in the dictionary is defined as "a strong surge of feeling marked by an impulse to outward expression, often accompanied by complex bodily reactions." When considering type, it is important to distinguish emotion (the visible expression of affect) from feeling, which is used to describe a rational process of making decisions. Feeling judgment can be mature or immature. Mature feeling insures that transitory pleasures do not outweigh long-term important values.

Feeling is rational, but not intended to be logical, since logic is the province of thinking.

12. b. extraversion or introversion. (This is called "orientation to life" because extraversion means "to be focused outwardly" and introversion means "to be focused inwardly.")

   a. Judging and perceptive refer to one's reactions only to the outer world.

   c. The dominant and auxiliary are mental processes which are used in the extraverted or introverted orientations (or attitudes).

13. a. judging or perceptive

   b. Only the extravert's attitude toward the outer world is governed by the favorite process.

   c. Only the introvert's attitude toward the outer world is governed by the second favorite process.

14. c. produce different sets of interests, values, needs, habits of mind, and surface traits

   a. The combinations of perception and judgment, when understood in type theory, give us a way to increase our ability to predict people's behavior.

   b. The "types" are produced by more than the combination of preferences of perception and judgment. Types result from the combinations of the orientation (EI preference), the dominant and auxiliary mental processes, and the attitude toward the outside world (JP preference).

15. a. facts which can be verified by senses and analysis

   b. and c. refer to activities more interesting to persons preferring intuition rather than sensing perception.

16. b. making decisions about facts which take into account how people feel

   a. Impersonal and logical handling of people tends to be more interesting to thinking types.

   c. Problems which allow use of imagination are more interesting to intuitive types.

17. b. possibilities for people

   a. The sensing plus thinking people are more interested in equipment and tools.

   c. Sensing types are more interested than intuitives in facts about projects.

18. b. are interested in possibilities which they approach with impersonal analysis

    a. Sensing people are more likely to enjoy fact problems.

    c. People with the intuition, thinking, <u>and</u> judging combination are often interested in executive assignments.

19. c. for both extraverts and introverts

    a. and b. It is important to keep in mind that, by definition in the theory, JP points to the process used in the outer world by all types.

20. a. for dealing with the outer world

    b. Introverts use their favorite or dominant process for dealing with the inner world of ideas. Consequently, the "best side" of introverts is not seen by the casual observer, who mainly witnesses the less-developed auxiliary (second favorite) process.

    c. Extraverts, on the other hand, use their favorite process in the outer world, and the observer sees the best of them at once.

21. b. a perceptive process, either sensing or intuition. (The J in the type formula indicates that the outer process will be thinking or feeling. For an introvert, the outer process is the auxiliary, so the dominant process must be sensing or intuition.)

    a. An introverted type with a P in the type formula has a perceptive outer process (either sensing or intuition). For introverts, the outer process is auxiliary; therefore the dominant process would have to be thinking or feeling.

    c. Introverts with a J in their formula could not have judging processes (thinking or feeling) as their dominant, since these functions would be used in their outer world and the introvert's dominant is used in the inner world.

22. a. a judging process, either thinking or feeling. (The JP preference points directly to the dominant for extraverts.)

    b. For extraverts to have sensing or intuition as their dominant, they would have to have a P in their type formula, since JP points directly to the dominant for extraverts, and both S and N are P processes.

    c. Extraverts with J in their formula could not have a P process (sensing or intuition) as their dominant function.

23. c. to help both extravert and introvert achieve balance, and to keep them from ignoring either world.
    a. *The introverts are less subject to superficiality than are extraverts.*
    b. *Extraverts have fewer problems in putting their best foot forward than do introverts.*
24. b. the raw material needed as a basis for judgment. (When the favorite process is a judging one, perceptions provide the information on which to make choices; sound decisions cannot be made without adequate information.)
    a. *Whether decisions are made quickly or slowly depends on other factors. For example, extraverts are more likely to act quickly or impulsively, and introverts after thoughtful consideration.*
    c. *Although it is true that the auxiliary provides a second line of attack when the dominant does not work, the statement would not be restricted to the types with a dominant judging process described in this question.*
25. a. steadiness of purpose
    b. a means of evaluating the worth of their perceptions and the uses to be made of them.
    (Both answers are correct. Perceptive types with insufficient judgment may spend too much time simply enjoying their perceptions and too little time in using the information their perceptions provide.)
    c. *Judging processes are more likely to speed judgment, not suspend it.*
26. c. can make contributions toward greater effectiveness (Not only must the less-developed processes be heard, but they can be a source of richness and growth.)
    a. *If the less developed processes are suppressed, they are very likely to express themselves in embarrassing and detrimental ways.*
    b. *The four mental processes are needed and used every day, for effective functioning. None can be ignored.*

27. b. a definite preference

   a. A high score does not necessarily mean that, because a process is clearly preferred, it also has been well developed.

   c. A low score does not necessarily mean that the less preferred process has been neglected. Keep in mind that MBTI items force a choice between valuable preferences, all of which are useful.

28. b. little preference between the choices (The votes are almost evenly split.)

   a. The MBTI scores do not give information about the development of preferences. They merely show the strength of the preference. It does often happen, especially in young people, that low preferences are found in those who have not yet discovered which preferences are more trustworthy for them. There is some research to show that low preference scores in young people can be associated with lower achievement in school.

   c. MBTI scores do not show that both processes are developed equally well. They show only that both processes are equally preferred. It can happen, of course, that both processes are well-developed; this possibility is more likely to occur in older than in younger people. Some people report tension or conflict over use of preferences when scores are low.

29. b. are the talents you can aspire to realize, and the warnings of what to guard against. (The talents stem from the activities of the dominant and auxiliary processes; the warnings concern the consequences of lack of development of the auxiliary, and also of the third and fourth processes.)

   c. are among the most useful learnings you can experience from understanding type theory. (These learnings apply to yourself and to your understanding of other people.)

   a. This answer is partially correct. The theory does assume that each person has some processes and attitudes which are more comfortable, and that these preferred processes suggest the person's best road to growth. The answer is wrong in assuming that nothing can be done about it. The essence of type development is in learning to use all one's processes in increasingly skillful and appropriate ways.

30. a. will have trouble with other types. (People who are of very different types may have trouble getting along, especially if they do not understand type differences. They can be of great help to each other if they learn to respect their preferences and their different communication styles.)

   b. can be of more use to you than other types. (Generally, people who are very much alike have little trouble in agreeing what should be done, but since they have similar abilities and deficits, they will be less help to each other than to people of somewhat different types.)

   c. will be easier to understand than other types. (Similar types typically, but not always, find it easier to understand each other.)

   a, b, and c, are all correct answers for Question 30.

31. a. by being sensitive to the other person's type
   b. by being certain that the other person is aware of your point of view
   c. to understand what it is that one of you sees and values more highly than the other

   (All three answers are correct. If differences are identified, understood and respected, they can be discussed rather than fought over.)

32. a. to plan more effective learning situations according to type
   b. by expecting people to focus on processes intrinsically comfortable for them
   c. to plan situations which exercise all the processes and give children broad choices in developing their own type preferences

   (All three choices are correct. Although all of us use all four mental processes, exercise both perception and judgment, and experience both the outer and inner worlds in varying degrees, we learn best when we can learn according to the strengths of our own type.)

Using Type Concepts in Planning Instruction

INTRODUCTION

Schools across the United States, urban and rural, big and small, report that students' lack of motivation for school tasks is one of the most persistent and perplexing problems. Student motivation is, of course, very complex, having its roots in family life, peer relationships and societal pressures that lie beyond the teacher's range of influence. But teachers do have the power to affect student motivation in some respects; and one key to that power can be seen in the type concepts.

Type theory suggests that we break down motivation into four parts, corresponding to the four dimensions of type:

1. The extraversion-introversion preference shows the broad areas of students' **natural interests.** Extraverted people are, by nature, continuously alert to events outside themselves, turning outward to pick up cues, ideas, expectations, values and interests. This inclination to scan the environment gives them a variety of interests. In contrast, introverted people naturally look inward for resources and cues, and pursue fewer interests more deeply. Attending more often to the inner storehouse of perceptions and judgments, introverts take a reflective approach to life, while extraverts take an active, trial-and-error approach. Of course, extraverts often do look inward and introverts often do turn outward. All four pairs of preferences described in this section refer to habitual, but not **constant** tendencies.

2. The sensing-intuition preference reveals basic **learning style** differences. Sensing students attend most often to the literal meaning they find in concrete experiences. They learn best by moving step-by-step through a new experience, with their senses as engaged as possible. Intuitive students' attention is drawn most often to things that stimulate imagination, to possibilities not found in sensory experience. Their minds work by skips and jumps, looking for patterns wherever the inspiration takes them.

3. The thinking-feeling dimension shows patterns of **commitments and values** of a student. The thinking student commits to activities that respond to logical analysis, where illogical human factors

38

don't interfere. The feeling student commits to personal relationships, to a teacher or peers and avoids situations where personal harmony can't be maintained.

4 . The judging-perceiving dimension shows **work habits**. Students with a judging attitude are drawn toward closure, wanting a clear work plan to follow. Disliking unsettled situations, they may sometimes lock into a course of action without looking at enough of the relevant data. Students with a perceiving attitude resist closure, wanting to keep all channels open for new data. Disliking fixed plans, they may sometimes postpone decisions, leaving much to be done in a rush as a deadline closes in on them.

By taking these four natural motivators into account in planning instruction, by working with them rather than against them, the teacher can better direct student energies toward learning. This chapter shows how type concepts can be used for that purpose.

TWO FACTS ABOUT TYPE AND CLASSROOMS

The Sixteen Types Are Not Evenly Distributed

The sixteen types are not evenly distributed in the school population. It is hard to estimate the distributions of types in the general population, since different occupations, and different educational levels, have their own characteristically different type distributions. The estimates given below are composites of Myers' data on students and adults. Data on EI and SN are much more consistent than data on TF and JP.

Extraversion 70% — Introversion 30%
Sensing 70% — Intuition 30%
Thinking (female) 40% — Feeling (female) 60%
Thinking (male) 60% — Feeling (male) 40%
Judgment 55% — Perception 45% *

This means many more students are ESFJ, for example, than are INFJ, and more are ENFJ than INFJ. The uneven distribution of the first two type dimensions, EI and SN, is a crucial fact for teachers, as can be seen in the diagram following. A typical classroom of 35 students would have this distribution of types:

---

*These, and other statistics presented in the chapter, are from Isabel Myers, **Manual: Myers-Briggs Type Indicator**, 1975, Consulting Psychologists Press.

39

I S 7	I N 3
E S 18	E N 7

(The distribution might be different for elective courses because students' type preferences often influence their choices of electives.)

School Instruction Fits Some Types Better Than Others

If a classroom has six times as many ES types as IN types, what does that mean to the teacher? The question brings us to the second key fact: most school instruction gives an advantage to some types and handicaps others. Consider these three descriptions; do you regard them as typical of school instruction patterns?

1 . Students work individually on their own tasks, each with his/her own set of materials or books. Quiet is expected so each one can concentrate and think through the work individually.
2 . When new concepts or rules are introduced, the teacher or textbook tries to follow a sequence of first presenting the concept verbally, defining it; then giving examples, illustrations and/or demonstrations; and finally (at least sometimes) giving students an opportunity to use the concept or rule.
3 . The main medium of instruction is words, spoken or written symbols. A student's successful manipulation of words in a dialogue or on tests is the primary way that teachers have of judging a student's achievement. In the case of mathematics and some science knowledge, the symbols of instruction are abstractions representing things other than words.

Are the three descriptions typical? Yes, so much that they seem to be essential. Yet they clearly favor certain types of students. The first one is a natural format for introverts, who prefer to do most of their work quietly inside their own heads. Extraverts, 70% of the students, really do their best thinking with their mouths open. Extraverts want to push a half-formed idea out where others can react to it because the outer world of people and things is the one they value most. The most natural setting for extraverts, the one in which they learn best, is one that allows them to think out loud and to act — that is, to do, make, move, produce — rather than to use words about such actions. The testing of ideas and skills in the outer world tells the extravert whether the half-formed ideas and skills are worth having. The introvert, on the other

40

hand, prefers to test ideas against private criteria, in the inner world of the mind – a process which is much easier for schools to manage.

The second classroom practice described above, that of presenting abstractions first and applications after, appeals to the intuitive's learning style, not to the sensing type. Abstractions, such as definitions, theories, lists of procedures and rules, help intuitive types get into a topic because they want to see the abstract meaning, the relationships to prior knowledge, the "big picture," before they take on new concrete experience.

An example from a student

A conversation that I had with a student at a diesel mechanics school will illustrate both points two and three above. The student was complaining about paper and pencil tests, saying he did much better with "hands-on" tests in the shop. "I think better with my hands." When asked to give an example, he told of being given a defective alternator he was to take apart, fix and reassemble. He was given a diagram to guide him in the operation. "I studied the diagram and studied it until I thought I would puke. I couldn't understand it. So I threw down the diagram. I took the alternator apart, careflly laying it down in a pattern. Then I saw the problem, fixed it, and reversed my pattern to put it back together. It worked perfectly." Did he look at the diagram afterwords? "Yes." Did he understand it then? "Yes, sure. It made sense then." To this sensing type student, the abstract diagram made sense as a map of the complex territory only after he first put his senses to work in understanding the territory. It seems likely that similar diagrams he encounters in the future will be more useful to him.

Probably the young man was an ES type. His best learning came when he could use a combination of senses, actively operating on the realities of his tangible environment. Note that he did not follow the prescribed sequence of instruction, beginning with the abstraction, the diagram.

Contrast this student's experience with that of an ENFP, a type with intuition dominant. He was totally unsuccessful in an auto mechanics class because the books were late. When the books finally came and he could understand the principles, he could then begin to understand the machines.

The skills of reading and type

How extensively are standard instruction practices biased toward introversion and intuition? No careful analysis has been made, but the bias is widespread. Probably the young child first encounters it in the teaching of reading. Of course, reading is primarily an introverted activity; it is done quietly by oneself. And it is fundamentally an in-

41

tuitive activity, involving abstractions—the printed symbols. But reading need not be taught as if all students were introverts and intuitives. The skills of reading can be and are mastered by students of all types, and they all can leave school with a positive attitude toward reading. Tragically many students are alienated by their first encounters with reading instruction. Type theory points to the probability that most of the alienated children are extraverted sensing types. There are data which indicate that the dropout rate is much higher among sensing children. Isabel Myers obtained type data from 500 people who did not finish 8th grade; 99% of them were sensing types.

What setting for reading instruction appeals to ES types? They learn best through action, with many chances to talk. Reading aloud with a partner is useful. They can be asked to recall a concrete experience that is worth recording, or the teacher can provide such an experience. If the child wants to report an experience to someone not present, he or she can dictate it and see it transcribed; this process demonstrates writing and recording as activities that are interesting and useful.

To the IS types, exercises such as reading "sight words" may seem like learning nonsense syllables; it is more useful to help them decode printed language through phonics and word attack skills. Many S children need explicit practice in matching sounds to letters until they have mastered them all and are no longer mystified by the printed symbols. When their first excursions into reading begin with putting sounds to letters (and letter combinations, such as TH and DR), they are more likely to experience reading as fun. Once the basics are mastered, sensing students will benefit greatly from exercises that focus their attention on the meaning of what they have read; interpretation of meanings requires the use of intuition, and sensing children are less likely to do this easily without careful teaching.

While adult reading is mostly a silent, individual activity, type theory suggests that reading should be taught to most children as a social process: writing together and reading aloud; sharing stories, writing scripts to be acted; quizzing a partner on vocabulary and spelling; teamwork in writing and critiquing letters, reports and newspapers to be read by people whose opinions matter to the writers; reading aloud to younger people or to anyone else who will listen; and any other such activities that demonstrate reading as a social transaction.

Testing and type
Correcting the biases of instruction that harm ES type children is perhaps the most crucial unrecognized problem of American education. No doubt the biases are largely unconscious, unintended. But most textbook writers are intuitives, as are the writers of standardized

tests. Most are probably unaware that their products reflect their **own** intuitive way of viewing the world, their way of approaching learning tasks. Writers of pencil and paper intelligence tests, also intuitives, most likely are unaware that their tests have a bias toward the kind of intelligence they value most, intuitive intelligence (manipulating symbols, drawing inferences, and the like). Considering the biases, there is no surprise in the fact that IN students as a group score highest on intelligence tests, followed by EN, IS and ES, in that order. The record of American education in the twentieth century is a record of neglect of sensing intelligence, an intelligence typified by the young diesel mechanics student who bypassed the prescribed instruction process and solved his problem his way...and the kind of intelligence possessed by the majority of American students.

PLANNING INSTRUCTION TO HONOR THE RIGHTS OF EVERY TYPE

Certainly, all students have a right to a learning setting that will offer them their best opportunity to develop. Type theory provides new insights into how to match learning settings to students.

This section provides a number of ways in which you can begin to understand the process of matching students and learning settings.

The first of these is an exercise entitled Four Work Settings. The exercise is made up of four checklists. Use them first to identify your own most preferred and least preferred work or learning settings. Follow the directions with the exercise. You may want to mark the checklist items lightly in pencil, so that you can erase the marks later and use the pages as masters to photocopy for use of your students.

EXERCISE: FOUR WORK SETTINGS

Directions

Step One: Put a check mark beside those items that are true for you, on all four lists.

Step Two: Go back over all four lists. Draw a circle around the check marks for those items that are *strongly* true of you.

Pattern A

I AM LIKELY TO DO MY BEST WORK IN SITUATIONS THAT:

_____ will produce practical results, useful products

_____ involve other people or take group effort

_____ let me work toward goals step by step in an orderly way

_____ are real and not just dealing with theory

_____ give me a clear picture of what other people are doing and what they regard as important

_____ have realistic schedules that don't expect too much too soon

_____ let me learn from first-hand experience, on the job

_____ let me use the practical skills and facts I possess

_____ give me a regular work schedule, but give me some variety and time to socialize, too

_____ let me work with concrete things, hands-on materials

_____ let me "think out loud" with other people

Pattern B

I AM LIKELY TO DO MY BEST WORK IN SITUATIONS THAT:

_____ make practical sense to me

_____ have a clear organization in them

_____ are practical and realistic

_____ let me know just what is expected of me

_____ let me work at a steady speed, step-by-step

_____ require accuracy and careful attention to details

_____ require patience

_____ don't have many surprises in them

_____ let me use my practical experience

_____ let me use my memory for facts

_____ let me think through a problem by myself before I have to act on it

Pattern C
I AM LIKELY TO DO MY BEST WORK IN SITUATIONS THAT:

_____ put me on my own initiative

_____ let me plan and carry out new projects

_____ involve other people in solving problems, such as group projects

_____ let me create new ways of doing things

_____ let me try out my ideas to see if they work, to see how other people react to them

_____ don't require a detailed accounting of how I use my time

_____ pose problems needing more attention to the broad picture than to details

_____ provide variety and minimize routine

_____ let me figure out how to put theory into practice

_____ let me make mistakes without penalties and learn from the mistakes

_____ challenge my imagination

Pattern D
I AM LIKELY TO DO MY BEST WORK IN SITUATIONS THAT:

_____ let me work in my head with my own ideas

_____ let me work toward solutions in my own way

_____ give me a chance to be creative

_____ let me set my own standards of quality

_____ let me work hard when I feel like it, and go easy when I need to

_____ don't burden me with too many routines

_____ have important ideas behind them

_____ give me ample time to think out my ideas before I have to act

_____ let me use my hunches and inspirations

_____ let me follow my curiosity

_____ let me work in depth on things of importance to me

Look back over your responses and see what patterns you find. As you may have discovered, the A list describes ES preferences for work situations. The B list, IS preferences; the C list, EN preferences, and the D list, IN preferences. You probably put the most checkmarks on the list that matches your type, and the most circled checkmarks on that list. Very likely you also put the fewest checkmarks on the list opposite your type as ES is opposite IN and IS is opposite EN.

Now answer three questions, to your own satisfaction:
1. Does the list with the most marks reflect work conditions that are usually highly important to me?
2. Would I probably work less productively under the other three sets of conditions?
3. Do the four lists apply as appropriately to schoolwork situations as to other kinds of work situations?

Most people answer yes to all three questions, including young people. Some adults spread checkmarks across two or three of the lists. Their maturity gives them the flexibility to work well in a variety of situations. Young people may be less adaptable, more polarized toward one pattern. For such students, attention to matching of schoolwork situations to students' types becomes more urgent.

If the 16 types are distributed in your classroom as they are in the general population, you may expect a majority of your students to choose list A, with less choosing B and C, and very few choosing D.

The four lists were written to apply to any work situation, not just to the classroom. They do not refer to "learning situations" or "learning style" because those terms call to mind the usual features of the classroom (lecture, workbooks, audio-visual materials, etc.), and those features make it difficult to look more broadly at learning situaitons. (Later in this chapter is a list of classroom features that different types prefer.)

You may find it helpful to go back through the four lists and respond to each item as if it were a question beginning thus: "In my teaching, do I typically provide learning situations that..." Be critical and mark only the items that describe what you regularly have provided for students. From this analyssis you can identify what you most need to develop.

The following paragraphs describe a procedure for planning instruction that begins with the four lists you have analyzed. When thinking about instruction plans, keeping 16 models in mind is difficult if not impossible. A good place to begin is with four basic models — IS, IN, ES and EN — as represented in the four lists you have just used. This approach does not abandon the TF and JP dimensions. Rather, it uses them as ways of making adjustments in the four basic models, adjustments to fit the needs of individual students, or of small groups.

Described on the following pages are three steps you may wish to follow in planning instruction with the help of type concepts:

1. Begin by planning for the needs of ES students, because they are the types most often neglected in instructional plans. This is your central plan. Check your plan by using the items of the ES list as criteria.
2. Develop alternative activities, variations from your central plan, that will appeal to IS, EN, and IN students.
3. Adjust the plans for TF and JP differences that you know will be important to individuals in the class.

Examples of Class Projects Successful with All Types of Students

Here are three examples of instructional plans that had a strong measure of concrete activity in them, that followed the three-step planning process, and were (predictably) successful with ES students as well as the others. Note that the teachers who planned and conducted these activities did not consciously follow the three-step plan, but in retrospect all the features of the planning process can be seen.

The greenhouse project

Sixth grade students in Jacksonville, Florida, became interested in the processes of plant growth and got the idea of building a greenhouse so they could house the number of plants they wanted to grow, and could continue growing them throughout the winter. Concrete activity was at the center of the plan: presenting the idea to the principal, a field trip to a local greenhouse, letter writing to obtain information about greenhouse construction, dialogues with a nurseryman, a businessman and a construction foreman (a parent), and maintaining a bulletin board related to the progress of the project.

Science and math became concrete and active, too. Students made charts and graphs for the plant experiments; plotted the sun's movement in relation to the school to help decide the best location for the greenhouse; made careful measurements and worked up plans concerning the size, shape, materials and cost of the greenhouse; and the plant experiments themselves had many active aspects. All the students wanted to be involved in some way in the actual construction work: using the posthole diggers, sawing, hammering, and stapling the plastic covering on.

In analyzing the events as they evolved, we can see the ES and EN students would be equally drawn to the active aspects of the projects. Virtually all parts of the project were performed by teams, with the more quiet and reflective activities coordinated with the active work. The library research on greenhouses and the sun's path, and design work would appeal to IN's, as would the plant experiments themselves. IS's would be especially attracted to the planning work, learning from experienced adults, keeping accounts for the fund raising and calculating materials needed and the cost of them. Probably the IS students were also the most reliable in caring for the plants and recording the outcomes.

The third step in the three-step planning process is to adjust instruction for the TF and JP needs of students. That procedure is described later in the chapter. The greenhouse project involves such varied activities that the teacher would have many options for accommodating the TF and JP needs of students.

The slum housing project

Some Nashville junior high school social studies teachers planned a very successful unit for students of their inner-city school. Many of the students had the ability to do well in school but most were expected to drop out because of what was termed their "defeatist" attitude. Most of the students lived in apartment buildings that were poorly maintained. No one knew the landlord; rent checks went to a realty company, and requests about repairs mostly went unheeded.

When the teachers learned about the housing conditions, they proposed a project for the students to find out more about the situation and to try to do something about it. Students agreed, without much enthusiasm at first. Investigative teams were formed. After preliminary planning, some teams took a questionnaire, a note pad and a camera to an apartment building to interview tenants and document the need for repairs. These teams kept records of how much rent was paid, what requests for repairs were made and when, and which were honored; and what repairs were still needed. Another team went to City Hall to find deeds and other documents that would show who the absentee landlords were.

After a file of facts, figures and photographs was prepared for each building, the students made an appointment with the landlord and presented him with the file. In two instances the file showed a very wide gap between the landlord's probable net return on his investment and the amount spent for maintenance and improvements. In several buildings, the students' project resulted in repairs and had other positive spinoffs. Some students and their families became active in tenant cooperatives and earned wages or rent rebates for helping to care for their building.

Besides learning something about economics and local politics, the students more importantly gained a sense of their own capability to influence "the system" they had thought to be mysterious and inaccessible.

As with the greenhouse project, the central events of this unit were active and concrete, and were sufficiently varied that all of the 16 types would find activities of high interest to them.

The aluminum can project

Three middle school teachers had planned a year's theme of human ecology. One activity, suggested by the students, proved to be especially rewarding — collecting aluminum cans to be recycled. It not only led them into the issues of finite resources and recycling, but the income from the sale of the cans paid for the cost of busing them on several field trips: to a plant making aluminum extrusions, to a power plant to see how electricity is generated, to a small company that built solar heating units, to a sewage treatment facility, and to a bird sanctuary. Among other things, students figured out techniques for saving energy at home and monitored their family's consumption of energy by charting the relative effect of various conservation measures. As they became aware of ecological problems in their community, the students also wrote letters to the editor of the newspaper and a group of them presented a proposal to the city council.

These activities were the more dramatic highlights of a year of study, and they were strong motivating elements for the more typical activities: use of textbooks, films, resource persons, library report work and some laboratory experiments.

The thread common to the three examples of instructional planning is the emphasis on making active and concrete experiences the center of attention of students. Other activities, more conventional to classrooms, are sparked in that way and take on new importance for students who are not natural academicians.

Using Type in Classroom Instruction

Of course, instruction can not always be planned to incorporate the action, variety, and concrete experiences described in these examples. Type concepts can also help you plan better instruction when you are limited largely to the classroom and media center. The table entitled "Relating Type to Instructional Strategies" was developed by Margaret K. Morgan, of the University of Florida. It shows the classroom learning styles for each of the 16 types. Note that in the table sensing types are described as linear learners, and intuitive types as global learners. Linear refers to the step-by-step sequential approach to learning tasks

The global approach involves intuitive leaps, seeking to see the whole of the task first. Also note the preferences of different types for various media of instruction. These preferences are confirmed by research reported by McCaulley and Natter.*

Drills and teamwork

Even the most routine aspects of classroom instruction (drill is an example) can be infused with some concrete action to make them more appealing. When drill on reading and writing and other skills is needed, the class can be shifted into two-person teams. Team members can choose each other (for example, by writing first, second and third choices on a piece of paper) or ask to be assigned to someone. Teams should keep the same membership for several weeks, with the teacher cancelling a team or changing team composition as needed. During team time, members can decide whether to, and when to, work together or separately; and how much time to spend in either arrangement. Some teachers give the students the option of handing in joint work or separate products. The point is that two kinds of accountability need to be maintained. Individual students are responsible for their own work, and are responsible to the teacher. Secondly, the team members are accountable to each other. If the team members have been taught the concepts of type, and if they know each other's types, they can use their understanding of type to communicate more easily in the process of trying to be accountable.

Adjusting instruction for TF differences

When the basic instruction plan has been made, in terms of ES, EN, IS, and IN preferences, you then can consider the TF and JP dimensions. You can use this list of "needs" that are usually associated with TF and JP differences.

T   Thinking types need order, if order is taken to mean that logic rules the situation. They resent order that is not logical. The teacher should prompt T's to take leadership in analyzing confused situations, to use their logic to make the situations orderly, and to spell out logical consequences.

Thinking types need to achieve, to have a sense of mastery, and they need intellectual achievement more than F's. This need is a natural ally to the school's objectives. Many **T** children don't

*M.H. McCaulley and F.L. Natter, "Psychological (Myers-Briggs) Type Differences in Education," in F.L. Natter and S.A. Rollins, Editors, The Governor's Task Force on Disruptive Youth, Phase II Report, 1974, p. 146f. Available from the Center for Applications of Psychological Type, Inc., P.O. Box 13807, Gainesville, FL 32604.

know what they can master, what skills they can develop to the mastery level, and they need very specific help in this. Without help, some of them will find mastery in anti-social behavior, because the need for mastery is much stronger than the need to please people—including teachers. For the majority of the T's, mastery is most likely to be found in mehcanical and technical areas, many of which are unfortunately unavailable for students to explore until they reach high school.

T Thinking types need to **endure**, to **persist**, to **prevail** in things they are committed to. They want to have the last word in arguments. They may choose the wrong things to persist in, and they often need help in identifying the values that really are most worthy of their stick-to-it-iveness. Teachers can avoid useless confrontation with **T** students by recognizing early signs of persistent resistance and redirecting the students' thinking power into careful **analysis** of the situation, looking for cause and effect relationships. (Teacher: "We seem to disagree. Tell me how you see the problem...Have you thought about it from this angle?")

F Feeling types need **approval** and **personal support** more than they need to achieve, to prevail, or to be "right." In some **F** students it is much stronger. Teachers who emphasize independent, individualized activities for students should be especially careful that they have not cut off **F** students from one of their main sources of motivation: the sense that their work is valued and appreciated. They want warm, not cool or impersonal acknowledgement of their work.

F Feeling types need to **be needed**, to know they are **helpful** to peers and adults. They are turned off by assignments that seem to have no particular value to anyone except themselves in some impersonal, remote sense (as with memorization of many facts and skills that are found in textbooks). Receiving the teacher's personal support and approval does not adequately substitute for the student's need to be helpful. So feeling types are most likely to profit from work in a harmonious group—when the task involves group members in helping each other, with a division of labor and shared responsibility. Examples would be group projects, tutoring, team learning and drilling with a partner. Projects that have a goal of being helpful to people **outside** the classroom are especially motivating to **F** students. They may even warm up to more remote materials if the human side is presented first.

51

ISTJ

Linear learner with strong need for
order (SJ)
Likes direct experience (S)
Likes audiovisuals (S); Lectures (I)
Enjoys working alone (I)
Likes well-defined goals (S)
Prefers practical tests (S)

ISTP

Linear learner; needs help in
organizing (SP)
Likes direct experience (S) Likes lectures,
audiovisuals (S)
Enjoys working alone (I)
Wants logically-structured, efficient
materials (IT)

ESTP

Linear learner; needs help in
organizing (SP)
Needs to know why before doing
something (S)
Likes group projects, class reports,
team competition (E)
Likes direct experience (S)
Likes audiovisuals (S)
May like lecture (T)

ESTJ

Linear learner with strong need for
structure (SJ)
Needs to know why before doing
something (S)
Likes direct experience (S)
Likes group projects, class reports, team
competition (E)
Likes audiovisuals, practical tests (S)
May like lecture (T)

ISFJ

Linear learner with strong need for
order (SJ)
Likes direct experience (S)
Likes listening to lectures (I)
Likes audiovisuals (S)
Enjoys working alone (I)
Likes practical tests(S)

ISFP

Linear learner; needs help in
organizing (SP)
Likes direct experience (S)
Needs well-defined goals (S)
Needs harmony in group projects (F)
Likes audiovisuals, practical tests (S)
Enjoys working alone (I)
Needs sensitive instructor (IF)

ESFP

Linear learner; needs help in
organizing (SP)
Likes direct experience (S)
Likes audiovisuals; practical tests (S)
Needs to know why before doing
something (S)
Likes group projects, team competition,
class reports (E)
Needs orderly, well-defined goals (S)

ESFJ

Linear learner with strong need for
structure (SJ)
Needs to know why before doing
something (S)
Needs well-defined goals (S)
Values harmonious group projects, team
competition, class reports (E)
Likes audiovisuals; practical tests (S)
Likes direct experience (S)

INFJ

Can be global or linear (NJ)
Wants to consider theroy first, then
  applications (N)
Enjoys working alone (I)
Prefers open-end instruction (N)
Needs harmony in group work (F)

INTJ

Can be global or linear (NJ)
Wants to consider theory first, then
  applications (N)
Enjoys working alone (I)
Prefers open-end instruction (N)
Good at paper-and-pencil tests (NT)

INFP

Global learner; may need help in
  organizing (NP)
Likes reading, listening (N)
Wants to consider theory first, then
  applicatons (N)
Needs harmony in group work (F)
Prefers open-end instruction (N)
Enjoys working alone (I)
Likes autonomy (NP)

INTP

Global learner, needs help in coming to
  closure (NP)
Likes reading, listening (N)
Wants to consider theory first, then
  applications (N)
Good at paper-and-pencil tests (NT)
Prefers open-end instruction (N)
Enjoys working alone (I)
Likes autonomy (NP)

ENFP

Global learner; needs choices and
  deadlines (NP)
Likes seminars (EN)
Likes reading if can settle down long
  enough (EN)
Likes harmonious group projects, team
  competition, class reports (EF)
Likes autonomy (NP)
Needs help with organizing (NP)

ENTP

Global learner; needs choices and
  deadlines (NP)
Likes autonomy (NP)
Likes seminars (EN)
Likes reading, listening (N)
Wants to consider theory, then
  applications (N)
Good at paper-and-pencil tests (NT)
Prefers open-end instruction (N)

ENFJ

Can be global or linear learner (NJ)
Likes seminars (EN)
Likes reading if can settle down long
  enough (ENF)
Likes harmonious group projects, class
  reports (EF)
Likes listening (N)
Likes pencil-and-paper tests (N)
Prefers open-end instruction (N)
Wants to consider theory, then
  applications (N)

ENTJ

Can be global or linear learner (NJ)
Likes seminars (EN)
Likes reading if can settle down long
  enough (EN)
Likes group projects, class reports, team
  competition (E)
Likes listening (N)
Likes pencil-and-paper tests (N)
Prefers open-end instruction (N)
Wants to consider theory, then
  applications (N)

F Feeling types strongly need friendship. They value harmony and will give in on disagreements because they want to preserve satisfying personal relationships. If the teacher will give them the opportunity to call attention to disharmony in the classroom, **F** students can be very helpful in leading the class toward an improved classroom climate. Most important of all to many **F** students is the opportunity to work with a friend. Friends who work together generally will stay on task if they know they will be separated when they abuse the opportunity. Peer affiliation is probably the most powerful force inside middle schools and high schools. The wise teacher harnesses it and doesn't try to fight it.

Adjusting instruction for JP differences

Judging types need structure and predictability much more often than do perceptive types. IS—J students need them most. If **J** students do not have their own structure for schoolwork worked out, the teacher must provide it. They value an **orderly sequence** of studies. J's can be comfortable with some variety and spontaneity if they know that an underlying structure is intact or that the structure actually calls for those things.

J Judging types need **milestones, completions, and a sense of closure.** Progress charts and tangible records are useful. Ceremonies, even little ones, to mark successful completions are valued, as are traditions generally. Persistence is a related **J** trait, and ceremonies that honor successful persistence will be especially appreciated. (In contrast, persistence does not come easily to P's, but they need to develop it. The ceremonies are likely to benefit them too.)

J Judging types need a **system of accountability** that is clear and made known in advance. They want to know what they are accountable for, when, how, and by what standards they will be judged. J's will learn out of a sense of duty, for a while at least; but that is not a good substitute for clear expectations made known in advance.

P Perceptive types need variety, novelty and change. As McCaulley and Natter note, the typically structured classroom "can make the perceptive types feel imprisoned, with the result that they spend energy needed for study trying to get freedom. More flexible classrooms are naturally more suited to these students."

54

P Perceptive types need **autonomy** and a **real choice.** the need is especially strong in _ N _ P types. They work much better at tasks they have chosen. They will accept structure and a system of accountability if they have choices within the structure, and especially if they have had a hand in deciding and protecting the structure. For example, a system of individual contracts, in which a student can negotiate some activities, is a structure P's would enjoy planning and supporting.

P Perceptive types need opportunities to be **spontaneous** and freewheeling, to follow their **curiosity.** The teacher alert to this need will find tasks for P's that let them explore and find new facts or possibilities for the class to use.

Exercise: Plan a Unit of Instruction Using Type Concepts

Here are steps you can take to try out the ideas of type in your classroom. If you have a colleague or two with whom you can share your plan, this planning sequence may be helpful to you.

1 . Select one classroom group of students with which to try using type concepts. As needed, coordinate your choice of students and your instruction plans with other people. Even if you do not think it is appropriate for your students to answer the MBTI, you can still use type concepts in many ways to reach students of different types.

2 . If your students are 12 years or older, decide whether to administer the Myers-Briggs Type Indicator to them. In most situations, teachers need to coordinate MBTI administration with the school counselor and obtain approval of the principal. If you decide to use the MBTI, precede the administering of it with and introduction to the idea, such as the "People Types and Tiger Stripes" activity in Chapter One. The introduction should serve to spark students' interest in the instrument so they will respond to it seriously. Some students will have difficulty with the instrument because of its reading level. Reading the items orally to them is an option. If you do read the questions to them, each student should have a copy of the Indicator to look at as you read. Tell the students the Indicator was created for grownups, and there may be questions where they do not understand the words. In this case, they may omit the question. Do not interpret questions for the students. If you read questions aloud, take care to make sure your own type preferences don't show. Make each choice sound equally desirable. After they take the MBTI, be sure they have their profile interpreted and their

questions answered. Nearly all the students will be keenly interested in their profiles.

3 . Decide whether to have the students respond to the four lists entitled, "I Am Likely to Do My Best Work.." Steps two and three are intended to give you some evidence of the types of your students. Having information on that is not essential to this planning sequence, but it is helpful. If you have students who cannot read the Indicator or the other materials, it is possible to recognize characteristics of type in their behavior. In the next chapter is a set of observation checklists by which you can estimate students' types by observing the patterns in their behavior. The process is time-consuming but it may fit your needs. Once again. knowing each student's type is not essential to planning instruction with type concepts.

4 . Prepare a plan of instruction — either a new plan you have not implemented before. or a revision of a plan you have used before. This plan will incorporate type concepts, following the three-step process described earlier in this chapter. Prepare it in sufficient detail so that your colleagues can read it and probably follow its intent without having to ask you for clarification on major points. If you prefer, you can prepare a joint plan with one or more partners. In either case, your plan should have a clear rationale based on type concepts.

5 . Decide what data you can gather, as progress reports or a final report at the end of the unit, to show tangibly how well your plan worked. If you do succeed in making a better match between students and the learning setting, what would you expect to improve? Student time-on-task can be estimated by simple observation. Student interest can be sampled by a few questionnaire items. Student achievement can be documented by student products and by teacher-made tests. Organize these ideas into an evaluation plan.

6 . Before you implement your plan, have your colleague(s) review it, critique its applications of type concepts, and make suggestions.

Developmental Needs And Type Concepts 3

Promoting achievement of skills and knowledge is the first goal of American schools. Helping students develop as integrated persons is another goal. The realities of schooling are such that achievement gets virtually all the attention and development gets almost none. One reason for the imbalance is that teachers have many practical models to follow for promoting achievement, but very few models for helping students with development needs. Type concepts, as yet unknown to most educators, are a practical resource that teachers can use to help individual students in their development.

EACH TYPE HAS STRENGTHS AND WEAKNESSES

Strengths and weaknesses in people, as shown by type theory, come in patterns. By analyzing students in terms of type concepts, you can get some insights into their strengths and weaknesses and get clues to use in planning ways to help them develop. Consider Lisa, for example, who was described in the Introduction to the book. Reread the two paragraphs about Lisa. Now that you know about type concepts, what type would you say Lisa is? Extraversion is obvious (talkative, gregarious). The friendliness and the desire to be helpful and popular strongly suggest a feeling process at work. The other preferences are harder to detect in this brief description. Here is a speculation. The easy rapport with others suggests a sensing-feeling combination. A preference for S and F is further indicated by her choosing to avoid complexities and her difficulty in getting an objective perspective on herself. Because she wants very much to be helpful and be accepted, but then misses the mark and annoys her friends, she may be a judging type—so intent on ends that she neglects the means. Since her own motives seem to her to be so pure, the hurt and resentment she experiences from criticism further support the feeling-judging choice. Lisa, then, is probably an Extraverted Feeling type, ESFJ.

Looking at Opposites

If Lisa is indeed an ESFJ, how does that identification help us think

57

about her personal development needs? There are two fairly easy techniques for starting the process. First consider the type that is opposite hers, INTP. In general INTP's strengths are ESFJ's weaknesses, and vice versa. What INTP does well naturally, ESFJ probably does least well. In *Introduction to Type* read the description of INTP (Page 10) and see if you think Lisa's weaknesses seem to be INTP strengths. When you examine the profile of the opposite type you can better see the pattern and range of the strengths and weaknesses of the type you are trying to help.

The Zig-Zag Process

The second technique for analyzing strengths and weaknesses is to look at the person's "zig-zag" process. Zig-zag refers to the sequence in which we use the four processes—S, N, T and F—in solving a problem.

The sequence begins with sensing. When faced with a problem, we properly start by gathering relevant, concrete data through the senses. The raw data by themselves do not settle the problem. The meaning of the data, their relationships to prior experience, are given by intuition—so the arrow goes from S to N. Intuition also asks: What are the possibilities in these data for solving the problem? The arrow moves from N to T when we engage thinking to analyze and decide the logical consequences of acting upon each of the possibilities. And finally the possibilities are also weighed by the feeling-judgment to assess how deeply we care about the effects of each option; we test the human consequences, the harmony with basic personal values, or the values of others. A mature settling of the problem will have involved the four processes in a balanced way. But, of course, each type plays favorites with the four processes, and balance is difficult to achieve.

In Lisa's situation, the imbalance favors feeling, her dominant process, and sensing, her auxiliary process (Remember? An EJ's favorite process is one of the two kinds of judgment—F in Lisa's case—and the extravert uses the favorite process in the outside world). So an ESFJ gives most attention to feeling and second most attention to sensing. Lisa's zig-zag would look like this:

$$S \longrightarrow N$$
$$T \longleftrightarrow F$$

The unbalancing power of her F is pulling her mental processes too quickly through N, zipping past T and coming to rest in a comfortable feeling judgment; but the judgment, unfortunately, is based on too few raw data (S), consideration of too few possibilities (N) inadequately analyzed (T). So Lisa seems flighty and her work is described as trite and shallow. A mature ESFJ, on the other hand, has learned to use all four processes appropriately.

Helping Lisa, an ESFJ

Lisa needs especially to give more time to sensing and then to develop her intuition and thinking. What can be done to help her? The first principle in a helping strategy is: use a strength to strengthen a weakness. The message or action of a teacher that will have the most influence with Lisa is one that will appeal to her feeling process, her strongest process. Her E_ F _ combination means she has a very strong need to be accepted, to maintain harmonious relations with her friends. The need impels her to be very good at friendly talk and maintaining easy rapport. How can she use this strength to strengthen her weaknesses? Here are a few ideas:

1 . Next time she is rebuffed by a friend, the teacher can ask her, "What was your friend feeling when she criticized you? What happened just before? What were you feeling just before?" The objective is for her to tune more precisely into clues about her friends' feelings, to sharpen her perception and to stay longer in the perceptive mode. The place to show her the value of improved perception is in an area of great importance to her—her status with her friends.
2 . She is likely to do much better schoolwork when teamed with a classmate friend whose perception is better developed than her own, perhaps an ES_P. The guidelines for two-person teams in the previous chapter should be helpful. Schoolwork that permits extraverting seems more likely to help Lisa develop her sensing more fully. If the assignments she is given require thinking and reflection (introversion), the teamwork dialogue should stimulate her to do both thinking and reflecting better than she would when working silently by herself.
3 . Some exercises for listening skills—such as perception checking and paraphrasing—would appeal to her ESF_ nature and would strengthen her S.
4 . She needs and will respond to honest praise much better than to criticism. She probably would receive and give attention to

positive suggestions when they follow praise but not when they are couched in criticism.

5 . Lisa probably would respond to values clarification activities that ask her to recognize values implicit in her behavior, force her to make value choices and have her affirm her values to her schoolmates. The teacher should select valuing activities that are not too vague and open-ended. Lisa is a J, remember.

6 . The teacher could assign tasks to Lisa that progressively require and reward greater amounts of commitment and risk-taking. The natural step beyond value clarification is commitment and action of the priority values that have become clear.

TYPE DEVELOPMENT ANALYSIS

The process used for analyzing Lisa's situation can be applied to anyone. Here are brief descriptions* of four more situations of students with which you can test your ability to recognize type and to prescribe actions to help the students' development. Read each of the descriptions (enclosed in a box), decide what type formula fits the student, and circle the appropriate letters. Then on a separate sheet, write a brief analysis of the kind that was done for Lisa, and identify several activities or teaching techniques that you recommend for helping the student. You can compare your analysis and recommendations with those which follow each box.

Case Studies in Type Development Analysis

Jan: A conscientious student who gets off target

E I	
	Jan is conscientious and hard working, but often seems silent and remote.
S N	She usually works very hard, but sometimes accomplishes surprisingly little. At times her work is totally off-target. She doesn't even try to make
T F	others understand what she's doing, or why, and most people have given
	up trying to understand her and leave her alone.
J P	

Jan sounds like an **Introverted Sensing type, ISTJ,** with insufficient judgment. Her remoteness suggests introversion and thinking. Conscientiousness suggests sensing and judging. That her judgment is poorly developed can be detected in her work. She plods along without analyzing her work (a lack of thinking judgment); and she does not

---

*Adapted from descriptions and analyses prepared by Anna Neurnberger.

tune in to other people's values, and may be unclear about her own priorities (a lack of feeling judgment).

With the hypothesis that Jan is an ISTJ, here is her Zig-Zag, followed by some suggestions to try.

$$S \longrightarrow N$$
$$T \rlap{\longleftarrow}{} \longrightarrow F$$

1. She will be impressed only by specific, detailed suggestions. Advice not carefully worked out will seem like meddlesome interference to this independent type.
2. Her perseverance can lend stability to the group. If she can see that the group may need her to help them keep on track, she may be more motivated to become an active group member.
3. Whenever possible, put her in charge of important routines, and arrange for her to work out the policies with others. Within the division of labor, help her obtain jobs that are clearly defined.
4. Peers should be encouraged to explain their motives as logically as possible to her, and expect that she do the same.
5. Role-playing simulations of how a communication should transpire might be helpful. She can play the part of the person trying to understand Jan — perhaps she can even interview the person who is playing "Jan."
6. Jan will be encouraged by small victories. Any small progress she makes in the developmental tasks described above should be given prompt recognition.

Dean: The class clown who doesn't pay attention

E	I	
S	N	Dean loves to entertain, and can and does keep the group amused and distracted. Consequently, his own basic skills are poorly developed, because he's usually "on stage" instead of at work.
T	F	
J	P	

This one is easy! Fun-loving, out-going, adaptable describe a **sensing, feeling, perceptive extravert.** Dean is probably an **Extraverted sensing** type, ESFP, the type which has more trouble with academics than any other. Of all the types, ESFP's are most attuned to the present moment. Dean probably does his off-task socializing because academic work seems too remote and abstract to him, and it fails to hold his attention.

With the hypothesis that Dean is an ESFP, here is his Zig-Zag, followed by suggestions to try.

1. If he is still having trouble with reading, check him out on phonics. If his background here is insufficient it may give this type particular trouble.
2. He learns by doing. The more sensory input he has, the greater chance he will learn. Whenever possible, lessons should be multisensory. He may especially like a variety of media. Demonstrations and pictures mean far more to him than words or writing.
3. A lot of talk is apt to confuse him. Keep instructions to him simple and to the point. Don't expect him to read between the lines or come to conclusions without help.
4. Whenever possible, give him the responsibility of acting as arbiter for conflicting factions, and team him with people who will help him draw conclusions.
5. Glasser's *Reality Therapy* may help him clarify his goals and plan alternative behaviors.
6. Of this type it is especially true: "I hear, and I forget. I see, and I remember. I do, and I learn."
7. Self-management and time management techniques will also enhance his judgment.

John: The tactless bulldozer

E	I	
S	N	John is hasty in voicing conclusions and he hurries on to new tasks before old ones are completed. Action for the sake of action seems to be his approach to everything. Although he often shows a lack of concern for the rights of others, he seems sincerely sorry when reproached about his transgressions. However, he seems to make the same blunders over and over, and his teacher wonders if there is any hope for him.
T	F	
J	P	

Since he is described as active, quick to voice conclusions, he is probably an **extravert**. His rush to reach conclusions shows that he is probably a **judging** type, but J's are more likely to finish what they begin. If his haste is due to an intolerance of complexity, he may be a **sensing** type, but if his hurry to new activities is due to having more ideas and inspirations than he can control, he is probably an intuitive. Neither thinking nor his feeling judgments seem adequately developed, a real handicap for a judging type. Because he has a positive attitude to work in general, a lot of energy and a desire to accomplish things, John has a lot of good things going for himself. His "life-field" listing, forces in him that work for and against his personal effectiveness, would look like this:

John's Life Field		
Forces for		Forces against
1. Energy		1. Jumps to conclusions
2. Interest in activity	John's effectiveness	2. Leaves work incomplete
3. Quickness		3. Behaves "blindly"
4. Desire for accomplishments		4. Seems purposeless
5. Sympathy for others		5. Behaves inconsiderately

With these data, it is hard to see John's type. His forces against (1, 3 and 5) suggest a lack of perception, and (2 and 4) a lack of judgment. It is quite likely that his teachers' inability to understand him is due to their being very different types. It is apparent that his education has not been effective for him. His teachers don't understand him because he himself is confused and sending out contradictory signals.

Planning to help John

John's teacher probably should begin with a plan which takes into consideration the possibility that he is an extravert in a judging life-style, and attempt to gather more data about his preferred processes. In the meantime, he will benefit from:

1. Learning activities which allow action and free movement.
2. Activities which have as their aim specific standards, criteria, consequences and products, which are made clear to him in the beginning.
3. Learning to state his own behavioral objectives when undertaking new learnings.
4. Being teamed with very perceptive types, who can also benefit from the collaboration.
5. Learning listening techniques, such as paraphrasing and summarizing what has been said.

6. Carefully outlining and planning each project in detailed sequence.

Bob: Trying hard but fearing failure

E	I	
S	N	Bob has little self-confidence. He almost never volunteers a response in class, except privately to the teacher, after class is all over, because he isn't sure he's right. He often undertakes projects of such complexity that failure
T	F	is almost certain, even though he is willing to work long and hard. It almost seems as though he were his own worst enemy and critic.
J	P	

Shyness and a preference for complexity suggest **introversion and intuition,** and the long devotion to undertaken projects is characteristic of the **feeling** types. Because his vision is broad, he is probably a **perceptive** type. With the hypothesis that John is an **Introverted Feeling** type, INFP, here is Bob's Zig-Zag, followed by suggestions for helping him.

1. Busywork is not for him. He must feel there is an important purpose in which he believes behind the work he does. He should do well with a contract plan in which he can choose some materials and activities for himself.
2. Teach him goal clarification techniques, and show him how to break his large over-all goals into small, component, sequential goals which can be evaluated independently of each other.
3. Teach him evaluation techniques so that he can objectively assess his own work.
4. His confidence will be bolstered if he is shown the evidence of real benefits to others which are the results of his own efforts, even though the results fall short of his own expectations.
5. Teach him to check his plans with an opposite type who will tactfully question him about details and sequences.
6. He will benefit from uninterrupted periods of intense work on a single project, and from frequent and sincere statements of appreciation and support.

Exercises: Analyzing Student Difficulties

Lisa, Jan, Dean, John and Bob had at least one thing in common: their achievement of school objectives was being blocked by difficulties in their development — what teachers in earlier times called character development. If you now have some students who need help as these did, you can follow the process shown in the analysis of Lisa's situation. Try the process with at least two students.

Steps in analysis
1 . Write a paragraph or two describing their basic traits;
2 . Identify their types (guess if you need to);
3 . Analyze their strengths and weaknesses based on type descriptions;
4 . Analyze their zig-zags; and
5 . Make a list of things that could be done to help them in their development. We suggest *Introduction to Type* as a resource for this task, particularly pages 4, 5, 17 and 18.

Activities That Teach Use of Perception and Judgment

Many teachers have also found that ideas for activities come to them when they scan a list of judgment and perception terms such as this one:

Judgment	Perception
goal clarification	communicating
values clarification	observing
managing time	listening
choosing	smelling
deciding	touching
organizing	summarizing
criticizing	imagining
analyzing	collecting (data)
empathizing	investigating

Both perception and judgment

classifying	applying (concepts)
finding relationships	designing (projects)
interpreting	evaluating
hypothesizing	taking risks

Examples of lessons that promote perception and judgment can be found in many sources. Two important sources are:
1. *Teaching for Thinking*, Raths and others, and
2. *Values and Teaching*, Raths, Harmin, and Simon (both published by Charles Merrill Co.).

65

TYPE DEVELOPMENT: AN
EDUCATIONAL OBJECTIVE

Mary H. McCaulley and Frank L. Natter

AUTHOR'S NOTE: The following discussion first appeared as part of a report entitled "Psychological (Myers-Briggs) Type Differences in Education." The Report appeared in the Phase II report of the Governor's Task Force on Disruptive Youth, prepared for the Governor of Florida in 1974. The full Task Force Report is now out of print, but the McCaulley-Natter study can be obtained from the Center for Applications of Psychological Type, Inc., P.O. Box 13807, Gainesville, Florida 32604.

Education requires students to take in something new, and to decide how to use what they have learned. In terms of type theory, students must learn to perceive accurately, they must learn how to observe, how to pay attention to the facts and details of their environment (i.e., to use their sensing). They must also learn how to fit experience together into new patterns, to see what things mean, to open up new possibilities, to use imagination (i.e., to use their intuition). In making decisions, students need to learn when it is appropriate to be objective, analytical, and to weigh the consequences of their actions (i.e., to make thinking judgments). At other times, they need to know how to use their own values, to weigh the relative importance of long range alternatives to themselves and/or other people (i.e., to make feeling judgments).

In type development, we assume all students need to learn good command of sensing, intuition, thinking and feeling. For each type, two of these processes come more easily and more naturally, and two are uphill work. Teachers who understand type can help students discover their own natural bent. Then, they can go on to help them develop expertness in use of the four mental processes — first, by stretching their abilities in the processes that come most easily to them and have the most intrinsic interest, and later, by becoming at least passably good in the others.

Furthermore, schools can help students learn when to use the four attitudes: When it is useful to extravert and pay attention to what is going on in the environment, and when it is useful to introvert and pay attention to the inner world of thoughts and contemplation. Extraverted children can be helped to extravert effectively, but to enjoy their own company and thoughts. Introverted children can be given more time to work alone and to go into depth in studies, but can also be encouraged to learn the skills of extraverting — in the interest of having more experiences to think about. Judging children can learn how to develop their sense of order into effective study habits, but can also learn when it is better to keep an open mind and to stay curious and receptive (remain in the perceptive attitude). Perceptive children can be shown how to develop their open curiosity about the world, but can also learn when it is better to stop perceiving and make a decision...

Different types of educators are naturally most concerned with the aspects of type development closest to their own type. Traditionalists (*sensing-thinking-judging*) are demanding discipline and the fundamental 3 R's. Humanists (*intuitive-feeling-perceptive*) are encouraging free (unstructured) school models with "open" classrooms and curriculum. Unfortunately, both camps may fail to see that no single approach will be effective with all types of students. Rather than downplaying the qualities valued by the other, both approaches could develop educational experiences to meet the needs of all types of students.

Jung's terminology may seem strange at first, but the processes he was describing are familiar to all good teachers. Behavior management looks at what the child is actually doing — noticing the facts (*sensing*) of his outer behavior (*extraversion*), and then finding a way to reward him (by giving something his *feeling* values) to organize his life (use *judging* attitude) in a more effective way. When we use reality therapy, we ask the child "What are you doing (use your *sensing* to see what the situation is), what really matters to you (what is your best *feeling* judgment on this matter), and where is this behavior taking you (what does your *thinking* tell you of the consequences)?" When we ask students in career planning "What are the other possibilities you might consider?", we are saying "What does your *intuition* suggest?" When we ask "What really matters to you in the way you want to live and conduct your life?", we are asking, "What are your *feeling* judgments on this matter?" When we teach children to be open about what they are really feeling, we are asking them to *extravert*. When we ask them what is the idea that prompts a given statement, we are asking them to *introvert*.

The point is that teachers and counselors are already trying to teach type development to students, though they do not necessarily use the terms or concepts of type theory. What type theory adds is an understanding of the road each person takes to excellence — which process will be interesting and easy for him, and which will be difficult. It is possible to use the learning activities of a school to provide challenges and problems that help all types develop, by busying their minds on tasks that engage all their abilities and not just on tasks they can do with half their attention, or while "spinning their wheels." As schools improve their capacity to help each type develop in its best way, we shall find less visible disruption, and less underachievement. More important, we shall be training a group of citizens who can effectively direct their lives, and who have learned to value the important contributions of all types of people to the complex decisions of a democratic society.

OBSERVATION AS A WAY
TO IDENTIFY TYPE PREFERENCES *

On the next eight pages are checklists you can use to infer students' types from their overt behavior. If the students you choose to analyze are not able to read the MBTI, the checklists are a useful substitute. Teachers who know type concepts and who know their students well can make reasonable guesses about their types. Even if your guesses are not entirely correct, you will still understand your students better, after using this exercise. The checklists reflect the work of Isabel Myers and other students of type. However, only the Extravert-Introvert lists have been field tested as an observation instrument in a somewhat different form. The lists do not constitute a type indicator instrument.

Directions: Put student's name at top and put a check mark in each box opposite a phrase that describes him or her. Comparing tallies of E and I, S and N, T and F, J and P can give you an estimation of the person's type.

---

*The author acknowledges with appreciation the contributions that Anna Nuernberger and Carolyn Mamchur made to this section.

STUDENT NAME

If your student is an EXTRAVERT, it is likely that he or she:

chooses to work with others, with large groups

plunges into new experiences

is relaxed and confident

readily talks over events and ideas with others

is interested in other people and their doings.

readily offers opinions

shares personal experiences

wants to experience things so as to understand them

is enthusiastic about activities involving action

asks questions to check on the expectations of the group or teacher

has a relatively short attention span

dislikes complicated procedures and gets impatient with slow jobs

is interested in the results of the job, in getting it done, and in how other people do it

eagerly attends to interruptions

acts quickly, sometimes without thinking

likes to work by trial and error

communicates well and greets people easily

STUDENT NAME

If your student is an INTROVERT, it is likely that he or she:

chooses to work alone or with one person

holds back from new experiences

chooses written assignments over oral presentations

performs better in written work than in oral presentations

pauses before answering, and shows discomfort with spontaneous questioning

asks questions to allow understanding something before attempting to do it

is hard to understand, quiet and shy; seems "deep"

is intense, bottling up emotions

prefers setting his/her own standards when possible

spends time in thought, before and after actions

has a small number of carefully selected friends

likes quiet space to work

works intently on the task at hand

works on one thing for a long time

prefers jobs that can be done "inside the head"

dislikes interruptions

may spend too much time in thought and neglect to get into action

71

STUDENT NAME

If your student prefers SENSING, it is likely that he or she:

is realistic and practical

is more observant than imaginative

wants to have senses fully engaged and satisfied

enjoys owning things and making them work

prefers memorizing to finding reasons

is aware of environment and changes moods as physical |surroundings change

learns best from an orderly sequence of details

interested in facts and what is really true

keeps accurate track of details, makes lists

is patient

is good at checking, inspecting, and precise work

likes to know the "right way" to solve problems

likes an established routine

enjoys using skills already learned more than learning new ones

works steadily, not in fits and starts

is impatient or frustrated with complicated situations

seldom uses imagination or has inspirations

STUDENT NAME

If your student prefers INTUITION it is likely that he or she:

seems to like something new all the time

is more imaginative than observant

attends more to the whole concept than to details

is aware only of events that relate to current interests

becomes restless, impatient with routines

is an initiator, promoter, inventor of ideas

sees possibilities that others miss

is quick with finding solutions

doesn't always hear you out; anticipates your words

likes to have and do things differently from others

likes problems that require new ways of being solved

dislikes precise work with many details

enjoys learning a new skill more than using it

works in bursts of energy, with slack periods in between

jumps to conclusions; makes factual errors

finds reading easy

readily grasps meanings of words and symbols

73

STUDENT NAME

If your student prefers THINKING, it is likely that he or she:

wants logical reasons before acccepting new ideas

tries to be fair; is impersonal, impartial

finds ideas and things more interesting than people

is more truthful than tactful, if forced to choose

is brief and businesslike

takes very seriously facts, theories, and the discovery of truth

takes seriously the solution of objective problems

treats emotional relationships and ideals quite casually

contributes intellectual criticism

exposes wrongs in the habits and beliefs of others

is offended by illogic in others

holds firmly to a policy or conviction

hurts other people's feelings without knowing it

has a low need for harmony

is upset by injustice

seems not to know how his or her own actions affect other people's feelings

74

STUDENT NAME

If your student prefers FEELING, it is likely that he or she:

is personal, likes warm personal relationships

is more interested in people than things or ideas

is more tactful than truthful, if forced to choose

is likely to agree with others in the group

thinks as others think, believing them probably right

finds it difficult to be brief and businesslike

takes emotional relationships and ideals very seriously

is offended by a lack of personal consideration in other

is motivated by others

may comply or conform to avoid disharmony

permits feelings to override logic

forecasts how others will feel

arouses enthusiasm

is upset by conflicts; values harmony

dislikes telling people unpleasant things

relates well to most people

is sympathetic

If your student is a JUDGING type, it is likely that he or she:

likes to have things decided and settled

is more decisive than curious

lives according to plans

lives according to standards and customs not easily or lightly set aside

tries to make situations conform to his or her own standards, "the way they ought to be."

makes definite choices from among the possibilities

is uneasy with unplanned happenings

bases friendship upon beliefs, standards and tastes which are assumed to be shared

has enduring friendships

sets up "shoulds" and "oughts" and regularly judges self against these

aims to be right

is self-regimented, purposeful and exacting

is orderly, organized and systematic

likes assignments to be clear and definite

has settled opinions

may be tolerant of routine procedures

If your student is a **PERCEPTIVE** type, it is likely that he or she:

is more curious than decisive

lives according to the situation of the moment

may not plan things, acts spontaneously

is comfortable in handling the unplanned, unexpected, or incidental

looks for new experiences, expects to be interested

samples many more experiences than can be digested or used

takes a "live and let live" attitude

bases friendships on propinquity and shared experience

takes on friendships easily; may also neglect, drop, and resume them easily

aims to miss nothing

is flexible, adaptable and tolerant

wants to understand things more than manage them

leaves things open

has trouble making decisions

starts too many projects and has difficulty in finishing them

postpones unpleasant jobs

welcomes new light on a thing, situation or person

77

Type and Teaching Styles 4

FIRST PRINCIPLES

Teachers and researchers who understand type concepts see ample evidence that teachers' types do indeed affect how they teach and what they prefer to teach. Much more needs to be learned about type differences in teaching styles, but research is already supplementing observation to provide some interesting facts about the ways different types of teachers behave in their classrooms. The facts below come from three main sources. The first is "A summary of Myers-Briggs Type Indicator research applications in education" by J. L. Hoffman and M. Betkoudki which appeared in **Research in Psychological Type**, 1981, Volume 3, pages 3-41. The second source is a study by the author with R. L. DeNovellis entitled "Correlations of teacher personality variables (Myers-Briggs) and classroom observation data," presented to the American Educational Research Association Meeting in 1974. In this study, trained observers recorded teacher and student behaviors in the classroom; the observers did not know the types of the teachers they were rating. The third source of information is research using the data bank of the Center for Applications of Psychological Type in Gainesville, Florida.

Teachers' Choices of Levels and Subjects

Different types of teachers are attracted to different levels of schooling, and to different subject matter. More S's than N's teach in elementary and middle school grades; S's and N's are about equal in high school; more N's than S's are found in college and university teaching.

The preferences in subject matter are predictable. S's are attracted to teaching of practical courses, N's to courses with theory. T's are attracted to teaching of mathematics, science and technical skills; F's to language arts and humanities, and also to counseling.

Similarities and Differences
Between Teachers and Students

Teachers are more likely to understand, and get along with, students of types similar to their own. Some students, who are not very secure in themselves, especially need teachers of similar type, with whom they can relate easily, and in whom they can find type-alike behaviors and attitudes to emulate.

More secure students need the challenge of being with some teachers who are unlike them in type, so that they can test and strengthen their weaker, less-used, mental processes.

THE TEACHER IN THE CLASSROOM

Type Preferences and Teaching Styles

Extravert-Introvert differences

Extraverted teachers are more likely to give students choices about what to study and how to go about learning tasks. Introverted teachers are more likely to structure learning activities through the materials they select for students. Extraverted teachers are more likely to be constantly attuned to the changes in student attention and activities. Introverted teachers are more attuned to the ideas they are trying to teach, and tend to center the control in themselves.

Sensing-Intuitive differences

Sensing types tend to emphasize facts, practical information, and concrete skills. Intuitive types tend to emphasize concepts and relationships, and the implications of facts for understanding larger problems.

Sensing type teachers tend to keep things centralized, and focus activities on a narrow range of choices. Intuitive type teachers are more likely to give a wide range of choices to students, and the teachers themselves are more likely to move freely around the room than their sensing counterparts.

Thinking-Feeling differences

Thinking type teachers make relatively few comments about student performance, and these are likely to be objective statements. Feeling types praise and criticize, support and correct, in words and by body language. Thinking types have students spend more of their time focused on what the teacher is doing. Feeling types have students spend more time in their own individual work. Feeling type teachers are

79

more likely than thinking type teachers to move from student to student, attending to each student in their individual work, and usually seeking some dialogue. Feeling types also seem better able to attend to more than one student at a time, in contrast to thinking types who typically deal with the class as a whole.

Judgment-Perception differences

The classrooms of judging type teachers are more likely to be orderly, with adherence to structure and schedules. Perceptive type teachers encourage more movement around the classroom, more open-ended discussions, and more socializing in study groups.

Student Reactions to Teachers' Management Styles

The classrooms of I, S and J teachers are likely to be quiet and orderly When students in these classrooms get off task, they are apt to daydream, doodle, and do other passive, withdrawn things.

In contrast, the classrooms of E, N and P teachers typically have more movement and more noise. In these classrooms, students have a greater voice in decisions about activities. When students get off task, they are likely to do so actively and noisily. The E, N and P teachers spend more time trying to get students settled down to work.

Structure and Flexibility in the Classroom

I_ _J teachers seem to need the most structure in the classroom; E_ _J's need somewhat less; I_ _ P's need even less, and E_ _P's need the least structure of all. In fact, E_ _P teachers often do things that will bring unpredictability into the classroom—encourage open-ended discussions, ask students to create projects, permit socializing in study groups, etc. Clearly, the amount of structure a teacher needs for personal equilibrium will suit the needs for external structure of some of the students in the classroom, and will not fit others at all.

What are the implications of these differences for instruction? It is unrealistic to ask teachers to change their need for structure. There are two alternatives to the mismatch between student and teacher needs. First, students can be placed so as to obtain a better match between teacher style and student need for classroom structure. Second, teachers can learn techniques for varying structure—techniques that permit them to meet more students' needs, but yet do not force them beyond their own equilibrium.

As an example of the latter solution, one J mathematics teacher was able to keep his natural style, but to redirect it more appropriately. He realized that his own need for order and control was resulting in overbearing supervision of his students. He redirected his need for order to an inanimate object — a chart showing all the students' names and all the sub-objectives of the course. He exercised his J by moving the markers on the chart as the students completed their tasks.

In another example, a P teacher, who realized he was too unstructured for many students, found the answer in individual student contracts. Students who needed more structure got more tightly-drawn contracts. He also arranged for election of class officers. Students debated and decided on a set of class rules, and the officers exercised J responsibilities by enforcing those rules.

Type and Questioning Styles

The kinds of questions teachers ask students, and the ways they ask them, usually reflect the teachers' own preferences for sensing or intuition. Sensing teachers are likely to start a sequence of questions with a request for facts and details; the responses they are seeking are predictable. Intuitive teachers are likely to start with questions that call for synthesis and evaluation — "What's the main theme (issue, problem) here?" "What are your impressions of...?"

Because intuitive teachers personally like questions that stimulate imagining and hypothesizing ("If you were..." "What might have happened if...?"), intuitive teachers may assume that all students like, or should like, such questions to answer. Sensing students are put at a disadvantage with these questions, unless other questions that engage sensing come before them. "What did you see happening?" "Which facts are most important?" "Why?" "Which facts give you clues why so-and-so did such-and-such?" This sequence of questions carries the student from the known to the unknown, from the givens to the speculative.

Sensing teachers may neglect to ask students to synthesize, to hypothesize, and to attend to the "big picture." Intuitive teachers may allow students to be too casual about the facts.

Exercise: Types and the Teaching Team

The combination of types on a teaching team makes a difference in the team's productivity, compatibility and flexibility. A good mix of types is a strong asset to a team. Look at the type table on the last page of *Introduction to Type* which is at the end of this book. Does your team have three or four of the columns (ST, SF, NF, NT) represented?

81

Three or four quadrants, too (IS, ES, IN, EN)?

Read back through the nine sets of facts about teaching styles and consider your own teaching style in relation to your type. Anlayze your own zig-zag. Do these analyses give you a new angle for looking at your strengths and weaknesses? Does the zig-zag give you some ideas of how to use your strengths to strengthen a weakness?

TYPE AND TEACHER-TEACHER RELATIONSHIPS

You are already aware of many ways that type affects the relationships between teachers. Type concepts can also be used to analyze the complexities of relationships and make them more manageable.

Exercise: The Green-White Conflict

Here is a description of a conflict between two teachers. Using type concepts, analyze the conflict and consider what might be done to improve the relationship.

Understanding the Green-White conflict

Two members of a teaching team frequently seem to have misunderstandings. Mr Green is often the "idea man" of the team, suggesting with enthusiasm that the team try this or that. Generally his ideas seem sound to the team, but in need of some refinement and attention to practical details. Mrs. White, another team member, is usually the first one to question Mr. Green's ideas, on grounds of practicality, and she states her position in such a blunt way that she sometimes causes hard feelings. At that point, Mr. Green "clams up," and his idea fades away without the team dealing with it further. Outside of team planning meetings, Green and White seem to get along quite well. Analyze the Green-White relationship by answering these questions:

1 . What types are Green and White (make a guess)?
2 . How can you explain the conflict in terms of type theory?
3 . Assuming you are a member of their team and felt a need to help them, what would you say privately to Green? To White? Write your remarks just as you would say them; put them in quotation marks.
4 . Do you identify with either Green or White more than with the other? Would you be comfortable in the role of peacemaker between these two? Do your responses to these questions relate to your own type?

The Green-White situation will yield many more insights if you can discuss it with a colleague or two. After you have discussed it, you can compare your analysis and action plan with the one below.

Possible actions for the Green-White conflict

Chances are that Mrs. White doesn't even know she caused hard feelings. She is probably an _STJ. Say to her, in private, calmly and plainly, "I think you came across too strongly with Mr. Green. I'd say his feelings are a fact to be reckoned with next time. Your knack for spotting quickly what is missing in a proposed plan is a real asset to the team, but I'll bet Mr. Green feels you never heard what he did say. He probably wouldn't be turned off if you said instead, 'Your plan might work if we figured out how to deal with this and this and this.' "

Mr. Green, full of interesting possibilities (N) not thought out completely (P) was hurt by the critical analysis (F) and retreated too quickly to withdrawn silence (probably I — an E most likely would have argued and defended the plan). Privately, you can say to him, "I expect Mrs. White has no idea that she caused hard feelings. She's blunt, but I think her bluntness comes from her logic, not from her feelings. She certainly isn't alert to other people's feelings the way that you are."

Mr Green "clams up" because he values harmony more than the life of his idea. You might say to him, "I think her _ STJ is abrasive to your _ NFP, but I would hate for those differences to freeze out your good ideas. Simply knowing that she is acting true to type might ease the friction for you. I think we can really benefit from her natural talent for homing in on missing details, or gaps in a plan. Maybe, if you have more details filled in next time, the team has a better chance of agreeing on your plan and we can go ahead with your good ideas."

Isabel Myers' essay that follows seems especially useful for understanding situations such as the Green-White conflict.

TYPE AND HUMAN RELATIONS

AUTHOR'S NOTE: The following section is quoted from the Manual of the Myers-Briggs Type Indicator*. In quoting it, we go beyond the uses of type in understanding relationships between teachers and students, and between teachers and their colleagues. This section is concerned, more broadly, with uses of type theory to improve understanding of families and of human relationships in general.

The effects of type in this field do not lend themselves easily to statistical verification but can be explored by personal observaton and experience. The conclusions reached from the writer's observation and experience are therefore offered as a frame of reference for the reader's own explorations.

Recognition of the type differences, when carried over into the field of person-to-person relationships, may afford a useful system for understanding others whose attitudes or actions seem unreasonable.

Type theory would hold that type differences yield differences in interests, values, and problem-solving techniques which may facilitate or handicap a working relationship between two or more people. Where two individuals interacting with one another are of similar type, there is a better chance of communication of ideas. Sensing types like facts; intuitives like possibilities; thinkers like logical principles; feeling types like a human angle. A good sound idea can be presented in any or all of these forms, but difficulties may be expected to occur if, say, the thinker attempts to force logical reasons upon a feeling type or possibilities upon the sensing people.

It has seemed to the writer that most people get around this difficulty by picking friends mainly from their own type column, a fact generally apparent if one enters his friends upon a Type Table. In marriage there is a significant tendency to prefer likeness to difference, especially on SN. But parents and children have no option. They are stuck with each other's types, for better or worse.

The type differences, and the resulting family conflicts, can appear very early. A six-year-old girl with feeling said in dismay after a week's visit from a five-year-old thinker, "He doesn't care about pleasing, does he?" Basically, he never will. He has to have reasons. The small feeling type will do things for the sake of "pleasing" but is quite unmoved by logic. If one expects to influence either, he must give him a motivation that means something to his type.

As individuals grow up, each type can profit by learning how to get

---

*Isabel Briggs Myers. Manual: The Myers-Briggs Type Indicator. Palo Alto: Consulting Psychologists Press, 1962/1975. By permission.

along with the other. The thinker is by nature impersonal and critical. He likes effects to follow logically from causes, and he forgets to reckon illogical human motives and reactions among the causes. In any disagreement, therefore, he tends to state his position bluntly, without concern for the feelings of the other people involved. The effect is to stir up antagonism which makes agreement needlessly hard.

Feeling types, on the other hand, set great value upon harmony and good feelings and are very aware of the likes and dislikes of the people around them. They assume that the thinker is equally aware, and resent his tactlessness toward others as well as toward themselves.

What the feeling types need to remember is that most of the time the thinker does not even know how people feel about things. He needs to be told, calmly and plainly, before trouble starts, so that he can count people's feelings among the causes to be reckoned with and act accordingly.

What the thinker needs to remember is that the feeling types prize harmony and really prefer to agree with him if given a chance. He should start every discussion by mentioning the points on which he agrees with them. If they can feel that he is basicaly in the same camp with them, they are ready to make concessions to preserve that harmony and stay in the same camp. The points of difference can then be discussed rather than fought over. And the thinker's logic and the feeling type's understanding of people can both be brought to bear upon the problem.

Clashes between the types arise out of the very fact that makes opposite types mutually useful to each other; the fact that each sees the side of the problem which the other naturally overlooks. For instance, the intuitive is by nature a thinker-upper; the sensing type a getter-doner. The sensing type puts his faith in the actual; the intuitive in the possible. When an intuitive comes up with a blazing new idea, his natural course is to present it in rough and sketchy form, trusting his listener to concentrate on the main point and ignore the unworked-out details. The sensing type's natural reaction is to concentrate on what is missing, decide the idea won't work (which it won't in that form), and flatly turn it down. Result: One wasted idea and much hard feeling.

Either type could avoid the collision by a little respect for his opposite. The intuitive should be realistic enough to forsee the sensing type's reaction and prepare for it, work out the details of his project, and get together the necessary facts in unescapable form. The sensing type on his part should concede the intuitive's idea a fighting chance. He can say, "It might work if — " and then bring up all the objections that experience suggests and ask, "What would you do about this and

85

this and this?" The intuitive then spends his energies happily against the obstacles, changing his ideas as necessary, and often ends with a solution valuable to them both.

When compromise between opposite types is necessary, the best compromise is that which preserves to each party the advantage he considers most important. The sensing type wants the solution to be workable, the thinker wants it systematic, the feeling type wants it humanly agreeable, and the intuitive wants a door left open for growth and improvement. People often go to the mat for a scheme as a whole, when what they really care about is one particular merit that could as well be incorporated into another plan.

Whenever people differ, a knowledge of type helps to cut out irrelevant friction. More than that, it points up the advantages of the differences. No one man has to be good at everything. He only has to be good at his own stuff and decently appreciative of the other fellow's. Together, thanks to their differences, they can do a better job than if they were just alike.

Introducing Type Theory Into a School System 5

by Robert G. Duch

AUTHOR'S NOTE: As more and more teachers and administrators come to learn about the concepts of type, many questions arise about ways to introduce these ideas constructively into school systems. We are just now beginning to learn how to put Jung's ideas into practical use. One person who has shown considerable ingenuity in helping principals and teachers to learn to use type is Robert G. Duch, Assistant Superintendent in charge of staff development for the Catholic Schools of the Diocese of Pittsburgh. Dr. Duch agreed to write this chapter, describing his introduction of type ideas into his school system, particularly the steps he took in the very beginning. His willingness to share what he has learned, in the interest of helping our readers with their own beginnings, is very much appreciated.

When asked to describe my personal experiences throughout the past three years in using the MBTI in my school system, I planned my response around three questions: (1) How does a school system introduce type theory to its administrators and teachers? (2) How do teachers begin to use it? (3) What are some of the ways type theory is being used in the schools?

The central office administrators of our school system had learned about type theory and had agreed that the ideas would be beneficial in any of our schools. Principals and teachers in our system have to come to expect that new ideas for school practices will be studied by central office personnel and introduced to school staffs from time to time. As assistant superintendent in charge of staff development, I designed a long-range development program for introducing type theory into the schools. The program emphasized the use of type theory to improve instruction and to enhance the professional growth of principals and teachers.

THE STAFF DEVELOPMENT PROGRAM

The design of the staff development program was based on four principles drawn from research on successful staff development:
1. The principal is the key figure in any school.
2. Any new system change gives the principal the role of implementor of the change in that school.
3. The school is the single largest unit for change.
4. The local implementation of staff development plans should follow a problem-solving process, using effort-saving strategies.

87

Introducing Type Concepts to Principals

Being familiar with the history of staff development in many of our schools, I decided that principals would need some assistance in developing their leadership roles for staff development. Thus, the plan included opportunities for principals to learn techniques of diagnostic conferences with individual teachers, and of collaborative planning with their faculty. To implement the plan, I trained thirteen educational consultants of our central office staff in type theory and application, in uses of diagnostic conferences, and in collaborative planning techniques. Each of the educational consultants is a general supervisor serving one of our thirteen regions.

Introduction to the principals

At a meeting of all elementary and secondary principals, the superintendent gave a general introduction to the staff development plan and invited the principals to participate in this project, in either the first, second, or third year of implementation. More than half the principals decided to participate in the first year of the project. The others elected to participate in the second or third years. The superintendent also emphasized the importance of the principal as the staff development leader of the school. I then gave a detailed explanation of the staff development program, and the time line for implementing each stage.

Workshop for principals

To learn about type theory, the principals gathered in regional meetings. At these meetings, all participating principals completed the MBTI, scored them, and received the description of their personality preference types. The principals considered their descriptions, and came to conclusions about the types that best described them.

I explained type theory, and described some of the possible uses of an understanding of types for the principal as the leader of the school, and for applications in the classroom. This small group approach provided opportunities for a personal and informal climate. The use of type theory to help principals "know themselves" was an important step in preparing them for leadership roles in staff development in their schools.

Diagnostic conferences with principals

Each of the school district's thirteen educational consultants were responsible for working with individual principals in their own region.

In one-to-one conferences with each principal, the consultant led the principal through the phases of the diagnostic conference model. In this process, the consultants modeled with the principals the process the principals would later use with their teachers.

In the diagnostic conference model, the first step was to identify a problem of interest to the principal. The second step was to identify objectives for solution of the problem. These objectives typically involved professional growth of the principal, professional growth of the faculty, and improvements in instruction. The final step in the diagnostic model was to consider the attitudes, concepts and skills relevant to the identified objective.

In the initial conference, the consultant and principal shared and discussed information about their MBTI types as a means of developing a relationship of understanding and trust. They discussed important personality type similarities and differences between them, and how their differences might be used to complement each other in their professional work relationship. The conference also gave the principal the opportunity to ask questions about type theory and to become more familiar with it, in preparation for using it with the faculty.

In the second phase of the conference, the consultant and principal discussed the professional needs of the principal and the teachers, and identified specific instructional needs. They then established objectives to meet these professional and instructional needs. In almost every case, the consultant and principal saw the relevance of using the MBTI with teachers as a strategy to help teachers pursue the various professional and instructional needs which had been identified.

Introducing Type Concepts to Teachers

Principals met with their faculties to identify and clarify objectives for staff development, and to plan strategies to reach the objectives. In almost every case, the principal suggested the use of the MBTI as a helpful step in pursuing staff development objectives.

CASE STUDIES

The following case studies describe the process of introducing and implementing type theory through the use of diagnostic conferences of the consultant and school principal, followed by the collaborative planning of the principal and the faculty.

School A: Improving Teacher Communications

The consultant and principal make initial plans.

After the consultant and principal discussed their individual MBTI reports, they proceeded through the steps of the diagnostic conference. The principal said that she and her teachers needed to develop more efficient and effective ways of communicating and planning collaboratively. She felt that teachers were stressed by heavy work loads, and by personality conflicts among some of the teachers. She identified the objectives of a long-range plan which included workshops on time management, stress, collaborative planning, participative decision-making, and a clearer understanding of self and others. The consultant and principal agreed that the use of the MBTI with the teachers could be a first step in this plan.

The teachers learn about type

Some of the teachers of School A joined the principal in planning for staff development. The teachers agreed with the principal's suggestion for using the MBTI, and they invited me to conduct a workshop on type theory and applications. The teachers were given the question booklets and answer sheets, and asked to complete them at leisure.

When I arrived at the workshop, I found some teachers apprehensive about what was to occur. To ease the anxiety, I invited al the teachers to participate in a game called "Room Design." I explained that teachers should form small groups of three or four. Each person would reflect silently for three minutes and design a real or imaginary room. Then each person would describe that room to others in the small group. When they returned to the large group to share a few descriptions of their rooms, the relevance of the personality type began to emerge. I called attention to the fact that some descriptions were extremely detailed; some were imaginative; some were matter-of-fact and realistic; some teachers gave global descriptions; some teachers showed their extraversion by stating that their rooms were designed for parties and friends; other teachers showed their introversion by describing a "me" room for enjoying solitary activities.

Teachers then received descriptions of their MBTI types, and discussed whether or not the descriptions fit—most found them accurate. I then explained type theory, and described how the ideas of type can be used in the classroom. One teacher, whose type had come out ISTJ, had considered the "Room Design" silly, and had chosen not to participate. He found that his type description was so accurate, so factual and so realistic that he began to press me for practical ways to use type theory with his students.

90

Follow-on activities by the teachers

The introductory workshop with this faculty was only the beginning. The principal purchased **People Types and Tiger Stripes** books for each teacher and, after they had read them, conducted more discussion sessions about type and its relationship to staff development objectives, i.e., more effective communication, collaborative planning, etc. I conducted two more workshops to deepen the teachers' understanding about type. They were now using the theory routinely to work through the communications problems that had previously interfered with teamwork. It seemed clear to me that their new appreciation of personality type—strengths, weaknesses, similarities and differences—had helped to bring an improved climate for personal and professional growth to the school.

School B: Motivating Teachers for Professional Development

The consultant and principal make initial plans

The same process of conducting a diagnostic conference with the consultant and principal was used in School B. The principal wanted teachers to see the need for on-going professional development. She stated the problem in question form, "How does the principal motivate the teachers to update their professional selves?" Her objective was to conduct individual teacher conferences, first, to help teachers recognize their professional needs, and second, to plan collaboratively for meeting those needs.

The teachers learn about type

After the principal held individual diagnostic conferences with teachers, many of them chose to answer the MBTI. I was asked to come and conduct a workshop for those who had chosen to take the MBTI. In the workshop, I explained the four patterns of work and learning (ES, IS, ES, and IN), and related the patterns to the ways teachers teach and children learn. I suggested that teachers might want their students to complete the MBTI for purposes of instructional improvement. This suggestion struck a responsive chord.

Using type with students

The principal and some of the teachers decided to give the MBTI to the seventh graders, partly because of attitudinal and discipline problems they were experiencing with six boys in that class. The sixty seventh graders were given the MBTI by one teacher who was familiar with type theory.

The principal scheduled a meeting for the seventh-grade teachers, the consultant, and me. We discussed possible ways to regroup the students to improve instruction, attitudes, and discipline in the classroom. With a mixture of interest, hesitancy, and skepticism, the group decided to use type data in regrouping the students.

A type table was made showing the names of the seventh graders in each of the 16 MBTI types. All six boys who were "trouble makers" happened to fall in the active, innovative EN types, and all had been homogeneously grouped in the slowest track since the fourth grade. We began to group heterogeneously, thereby eliminating the track system. The children were assigned to three sections, more or less similar in type distribution; two of the "trouble makers" were assigned to each section. Each class had a range of student performance scores. Close friends were placed in the same section, if they had been together in the past. The groupings resulted in three sections, relatively similar to each other, except for the specialized classes in math and reading.

The regroupings occurred a year ago. I can now report that positive changes have taken place in the seventh-grade classrooms. All the teachers indicated that class discipline problems have "just about disappeared." The teachers are using type to broaden the variety of their teaching methods. Student attitudes about school have improved. The principal now reports that other teachers in the school are following the lead of the seventh-grade group.

Other Examples of Introducing Type into the School System

Student Council

Moderators of high school student councils are using the MBTI to help students understand themselves and each other. Student council members discuss their individual and collective strengths, weaknesses, similarities and differences, and use the information to improve their effectiveness in planning and achieving council goals.

Teachers change testing techniques

Some teachers are redesigning student tests to accommodate the learning patterns of students. For instance, more teachers are taking the time to give oral tests to extraverted students; they find significantly better performance in test results.

Type in counseling activities

After I had conducted a workshop for one high school faculty , a guidance counselor became interested and knowledgeable in type theory. She administered the MBTI to 126 sophomore students and discussed type with them in guidance classes. She found that many students who were reporting learning difficulties in certain classes were very different in type from their teachers. She also discovered that a large proportion of the students regarded as "disruptive" were the active, practical ES types.

In conclusion, my experiences in introducing and using type theory have been rewarding, personally and professionally. I have learned that school districts, schools, and individuals can use type theory when it is perceived as directly related to their needs, when school administrators and teachers collaborate on implementing the theory in concrete ways, and when it is used to help people solve professional and personal problems.

More than anything else, type theory helps in the understanding of how different learners experience instruction. In Kierkegarrd's words, "Instruction begins when you, the teacher, learn from the learner, put yourself in his place so that you may understand what he learns, and the way he understands it..." (**The Journals,** 1854, p. 29)

Taking Type Into Account in Education

by Isabel Briggs Myers

AUTHOR'S NOTE: The following essay by Isabel Briggs Myers was written in October, 1971, to describe how type theory can be used to understand the learning of children from their early years in school. Isabel Myers was always very concerned with the fact that many children are taught, very early, in ways which make them lose confidence in themselves, and cause them to come to hate school. She gave permission to share her thoughts here, and they make a fitting final chapter to this book.

Schools are being told that they are accountable for educating every child. They are required to teach the basic skills, so that every child grows up able to read, write and balance a checkbook. And they are required to plant various sorts of knowledge, deeply enough so that it will germinate, take root and bear fruit.

Both demands are better met if the schools take into account the type differences among children. These are not quantitative differences that can be expressed simply as a higher or lower degree of mental ability. They are qualitative differences, differences as to the kind of perception and the kind of judgment that the child prefers to use. It is his preferences that make his type. Children of different types have a different "mix" of abilities, different needs, interests and motivations, and different degrees of success in school.

The preference that has the most conspicuous consequences in education is the choice between the two kinds of perception, the choice between sensing and intuition. Sensing focuses interest and attention upon the concrete reality that is apparent to the five senses. Sensing children are more interested in doing something, almost anything, with almost any tangible object, than in listening to what anyone is saying unless it has to do with action or adds something definite to their picture of the physical world. In contrast, intuition focuses interest and attention upon the end results of one's own unconscious processes, which include the translation of symbols-words into meaning, and meaning into words. Intuitive children thus tend to take a positive interest in language, spoken or written, and acquire a facility that is convenient in class and in verbal ability tests and also enables them to state clearly and usefully to themselves the relationships and possibilities suggested by their intuition.

94

It is therefore understandable that, as most schools are now run, sensing children have less use for school than intuitive children do (often no use at all), that on the average they make lower grades and score lower on intelligence tests (though not enough lower to account for their grades), and that they far more frequently drop out.

If we are to have a system of universal education that does justice to all the types, I think we must draw a sharp distinction between skills and knowledge. Knowledge spreads over a tremendous variety of subjects, each of which may be interesting and useful to certain types and a waste of time to others. But the basic skills are essential for all the types, and should be taught in such a way as to give every child what he needs.

The usual first grade has a substantial majority of sensing children and a smaller number of intuitives. The sensing children do not want to have to cope with anything unexplainable. The intuitives do not want to be bored by anything tedious and dull. Except for an occasional child who may have been let into the secret by an intuitive parent or have found it out for himself, none of the children, sensing or intuitive, know that letters stand for sounds.

In most first grades, nobody (for a long time) tells them this one crucial fact that makes sense of the process of learning to read. Reading thus consists of memorizing "sight words", recognizable only by their general shape. A new word is an insoluble mystery until teacher tells you what it is. Content is necessarily restricted to repetition of the few words thus far memorized. "Dick. See Dick. See Dick run." This method of teaching manages to frustrate both the sensing children and the intuitives. Reading, which ought to be a magical extension of one's own experience, is both unexplainable **and** dull.

To meet the needs of the sensing children who want things to be explicit and the intuitive children who want unlimited possibilities, first grades should introduce intensive phonics at the very beginning, so that every child in the class knows that there is a perfectly good way to tell what new words are. He is going to be able to read, very soon, up to the limits of his speaking vocabulary. And removal of the artificial limits on vocabulary means that he can read vastly more interesting things. He can, in fact, attempt anything he cares to tackle.

From the standpoint of the child's success in school and his development as a person, with ambition, initiative, and confidence in himself, the start of first grade marks a crucial fork in the road. That is the point at which he decides either that school makes sense or that it does not, that it is interesting or boring, that he can or cannot do these new things. If he cannot do the new things, his only defense against the humiliation of being "dumb" is to decide that such things are not worth doing.

95

The pitfall in the teaching of arithmetic skills is basically the same as the pitfall in teaching reading. The children who try to cope with the symbols without recognizing the realities these stand for are doomed to frustration. They never win through to the beautiful certainties in the realm of numbers. They just memorize incantations. "7 and 5 is 12." "11 minus 4 is 7." "5 times 7 is 35." When the teacher gives you the first two numbers of an incantation, you have to remember the third. If you forget that third number, there is nothing you can do about it. And if you are given a problem and can't see what kind of incantation to use, there is nothing you can do about that.

The solution is to establish the reality of numbers first. The symbols then can be understood as a way of talking about reality. There should be no operations with disembodied numerals, no incantations, no memorizing, no flash cards for "addition facts" and "subtraction facts", no verbal drill, until the children are thoroughly familiar with manual operations with quantities. To many sensing children, things you can touch and move are real but words are not.

The form in which a question is put can change the whole spirit of the proceedings. "How much is 7 and 5?" implies that the child ought to know by this time and the teacher wants to find out whether he does or not. This is wrong side to. The child is the one who should be doing the finding out. "Find out how much is 7 and 5!" is an invitation to action. Using number blocks, for instance, the child can take a block that is seven squares high and stand it against the number tower. Naturally it reaches to seven. Then he can take a block that is five squares high and stack it on top of the seven. Together they reach to twelve. Every time he does it they reach to twelve. In fact, he can see that they have to reach to twelve; the seven block is always three squares short of ten; the first three squares of the five block always get you to ten; the other two squares always stick up beyond ten and reach to twelve. A similar certainty has to exist in the case 17 and 5, 27 and 5, and so on up.

Consistent use of this approach gives the child a picture of the number system as a whole, the place of any given number in that system, and its relation to other numbers. When he starts doing operations with numerals instead of blocks, he knows the quantities they stand for and what he is doing with those quantities. And when he is given a problem, he has a decent chance of seeing what he must do to solve it.

Reading, writing and arithmetic are well-defined skills that every child needs to acquire. But knowledge, as distinguished from skills, is another matter. It has no limits. Schools must decide what tiny fraction they will try to teach. If we take it as axiomatic that a child should be taught things that are of lasting benefit to him, either by making him more effective or by otherwise enhancing his life, one brutal conclusion follows. There is no use in teaching a child things he intends to forget.

Nothing will stick in a child's mind long enough to do him any good unless it interests him, and here type plays a major role. The combination of a child's preferred kind of perception and his preferred kind of judgment tends to concentrate his interest in fields where these find scope, as shown in the comparison on page three of the *Introduction to Type*. His remaining preferences influence the kind of work he will like to do in those fields. Hence knowledge that is relevant, even illuminating, for a person with a given set of preferences can be acutely boring to a person with the opposite set. Aside from routine warnings against common dangers, like carbon monoxide and the signing of documents unread, there is probably no body of knowledge that can profitably be "taught" to every child regardless.

Time and effort spent in trying to teach a child something against his own will are worse than wasted. Real harm is done. If a child is not interested in what he is supposed to be learning, he is bored. And the habit of being bored is disastrous for children, because it destroys their native curiosity. Babies and pre-schoolers have a great urge to make sense of the world. They devote their energies happily to finding out one thing after another, whatever fixes their curiosity at the moment. They learn at a tremendous rate, and they remember what they learn, because it becomes a part of their world as they know it. Learning is high adventure, not a chore.

School should be a continuation of the adventure. Children in all the grades should be given maximum opportunity to learn the things that have meaning and interest for them in terms of their own kind of perception and their own kind of judgment. To the extent that they are given this opportunity, they gain not only in interest but in application and intelligence as well. People of any age, from six to sixty, apply themselves with greater vigor to the task in hand when they are interested. People of any age are more intelligent when they are interested than when they are bored.

A child permitted to study what interests him learns more and remembers it. The most valuable outcome, however, is the effect upon the development of his perception and judgment. A purposeful finding out about almost anything develops his perception. And a self-imposed doing of whatever is necessary to that end develops his judgment far more than would mere obedience to a teacher's authority. The lifelong importance of adequate development of perception and judgment is shown in past and current studies with the Type Indicator. Good perception and judgment are associated with achievement, which is reasonable because they make a person more effective in whatever he sets out to do. They are also associated with mental and physical health, which again is reasonable because they enable a person to cope more competently with his problems and thus lessen or eliminate strain.

Ways of making room for individual interests and study can be worked out in any school where authority will accept the idea. In fact, they can be worked out independently by any teacher. A seminar approach can be taken, in which the class is given a bird's-eye view of the different aspects of the subject and then allowed to sign up to work on whichever aspect each finds most interesting. Or a list of individual projects can be designed to appeal to widely different types. Flexibility can be achieved by framing some exam questions for sensing types, others for intuitives, everyone being permitted to leave out the two he likes least. Or it may be announced in advance that everyone may formulate and answer one question of his own, substituting it for one not in his field.

Where students are old enough to take the Type Indicator, as in 7th to 12th grades, their types can be ascertained, subject to confirmation by the students themselves. Teachers can then learn by direct observation how their subjects need to be presented in order to catch the interest of ST, SF, NF, and NT types respectively, and can share their findings with other teachers. Feedback to the students about their types can add to their understanding of themselves and others, can reassure them that it is all right to be the kind of person they are, and can relieve the strain of personal conflicts at home or elsewhere by showing how these arise from differences in type. It can even help them to develop their perception and judgment. Page four of the *Introduction to Type* has instructions how to do it, exercising each kind of perception and each kind of judgment, separately, in turn, to find out what each can contribute to the solution of a problem.

Children in lower grades can also practice using the different kinds of perception and judgment one at a time in appropriate ways. Exact observation will exercise sensing. Figuring out possible ways to solve a difficulty will exercise intuition. Thinking out all the unintended consequences that may result from an action will exercise thinking. Weighing how other people will feel about things will exercise feeling.

An early clue to a child's type may be obtainable from his response to these activities. The sensing child should find the sensing exercise easier and more fun than the intuitive exercise. The little thinker will prefer thinking about consequences to guessing about other people's feelings. And so on. An observant teacher may be able to draw useful inferences as to the way each child's mind works and what will help him most. Whether she does or not, the children will benefit directly from practice in these four different, important ways of using their minds.

EPILOGUE

NEXT STEPS IN USING TYPE CONCEPTS

In this book I have described the concepts of type. I have tried to show you how to understand your own type, and how to use it in working with students and colleagues. Many people have shared in the ideas described in this book. Many more people are finding creative and practical ways to make teaching more rewarding and learning more efficient.

We hope you will want to learn more about the uses of type theory, and will share what you learn with other people. The following suggestions are designed to help you with both these endeavors.

Isabel Myers' book, **Gifts Differing**, is the most important resource for a deeper understanding of type. I believe it will become an American classic. It can be ordered from Consulting Psychologists Press or from the Center for Applications of Psychological Type. (Both addresses are given below.)

The following organizations provide resources for using the ideas about type:

> The **Center for Applications of Psychological Type, Inc.** (CAPT), which Isabel Myers helped to found before her death, is a non-profit organization for research, publication and training in the uses of type theory. CAPT publishes and distributes books, reports, and training materials related to type. Its staff conducts workshops around the country for counselors, educators, and other professionals who wish to improve their understanding of type for working with students, clients, and organizations. CAPT publishes a bibliography of MBTI research and maintains a library of published and unpublished materials on type. The CAPT data bank of over 150,000 cases, derived from computer scoring of the MBTI, is used to learn more about the attractiveness of occupations to each of the types. The address of CAPT is P.O. Box 13807, Gainesville, Florida 32604, and the telephone number is (904) 375-0160.

The **Association for Psychological Type** (APT) is a membership organization formed in 1979 at the Third National Conference of users of the MBTI. APT membership is open to all persons interested in type. APT is developing a number of ways of spreading knowledge about type. It is creating local chapters whose members meet to "talk type." Regional meetings and national conferences allow for much formal and informal information sharing. APT also shares ideas through its newsletter, *MBTI News*, and through a journal, **Research in Psychological Type**. APT members join one or more interest areas—Careers and Occupations, Counseling, Education, Management and Organizational Development, Psychological Theory, Religious Issues, and Research. For information or a membership application, write the APT Membership Secretary, P.O. Box 13807, Gainesville, Florida 32604.

Consulting Psychologists Press (CPP) is the publisher of the Myers-Briggs Type Indicator, **Gifts Differing**, and *Introduction to Type*. Psychologists, counselors, and others professionally qualified to purchase psychological tests can order the MBTI from CPP, and anyone may order other books and materials related to type. The **MBTI Manual** is, of course, an essential resource. The address of CPP is 577 College Avenue, Palo Alto, CA 94306. The telephone number is (415) 857-1444.

We encourage you to go further in your exploration and applications of psychological type, and hope you will share your discoveries with us, to enrich future editions of this book.

Gordon D. Lawrence

APPENDIX

INTRODUCTION TO TYPE

ISABEL BRIGGS MYERS

CONSULTING PSYCHOLOGISTS PRESS, INC.
577 College Avenue, Palo Alto, CA 94306

CONTENTS

FOREWORD

The questions in the Myers-Briggs Type Indicator are not important in themselves, but they do indicate basic preferences that have far-reaching effects. There is no right or wrong to these preferences. They simply produce different kinds of people who are interested in different things, are good in different fields and often find it hard to understand each other.

People with preferences opposite to yours tend to be opposite to you in many ways. They are likely to be weak where you are strong, and strong where you are weak. Each type has its own set of strengths and abilities.

An understanding of type in general and your own type in particular can help you choose your career. It can also help you deal with the problems and people in your life. The following pages provide a number of ways for you to explore your own preferences and verify your own type. The Indicator reports your type by four letters that show how you came out on each of the four preferences. You can check these letters against the explanations of the separate preferences (pages 2 and 6), the effects of the combinations of perception and judgment (page 3), the effects of the combinations of all four preferences in young people (pages 7-8), the adult descriptions (pages 9-16), and the effects of each preference in work situations (pages 17-18).

If the description of your reported type makes you feel comfortably understood, your four letters are probably right. If it does not fit you, one or more of the letters may be wrong. Sometimes people are not sure what they do prefer, or they disown their real preference for fear they ought to prefer the opposite, or their answers are affected by chance factors. If your reported type does not seem right to you, read the descriptions for the types that differ from it by a letter or two, and see which one comes closest to being a satisfactory description of yourself.

ISBN: 0-935652-06-x

OPPOSITE KINDS OF PERCEPTION AND JUDGMENT

The Type Indicator is concerned with the valuable differences in people that result from the way they like to perceive and the way they like to judge. Succeeding at anything takes both perception and judgment. First you have to find out what the problem or situation is and what are the various things you might do about it. Then you have to decide which to do. Finding out is an exercise of perception. Deciding is an exercise of judgment. You have two basic ways of finding out and two basic ways of deciding.

Opposite ways of finding out: sensing and intuition. One way to find out is through your sensing (S). Your eyes and ears and other senses tell you what is actually there and actually happening. Sensing is especially useful for gathering the facts of a situation. The other way to find out is through your intuition (N) which shows you meanings and relationships and possibilities that are beyond the reach of your senses. Intuition is especially useful for seeing what you might do about a situation. You use both sensing and intuition, of course, but not both at once and not, in most cases, with equal liking.

If you like sensing better than intuition, you make more use of sensing, get to be more skillful with it, and grow expert at noticing all the observable facts. You tend to become realistic, practical, observant, fun-loving, and good at remembering a great number of facts and working with them.

If you like intuition better than sensing, you make more use of intuition, get to be more skillful with it, and grow expert at seeing a new possibility or solution. You tend to value imagination and inspirations, and to become good at new ideas, projects and problem-solving.

Opposite ways of deciding: thinking and feeling. One way to decide is through your thinking (T). Thinking predicts the logical result of any particular action you may take. Then it decides impersonally, on the basis of cause and effect. The other way to decide is through your feeling (F). Feeling takes into account anything that matters or is important to you or to other people (without requiring that it be logical), and decides on the basis of personal values. You use both thinking and feeling, of course, but not both at once and not, in most cases, with equal confidence.

If you trust thinking more than feeling and use it more, you grow to be most skillful in dealing with that part of the world which behaves logically (like machinery) with no unpredictable human reactions. You yourself tend to become logical, objective and consistent, and to make your decisions by analyzing and weighing the facts, including the unpleasant ones.

If you trust and use feeling more than thinking, you grow most skillful in dealing with people. You tend to become sympathetic, appreciative and tactful and to give great weight, when making any decisions, to the personal values that are involved, including those of other people.

The kind of perception you prefer to use, either sensing or intuition, can team up with whichever kind of judgment you prefer to use, either thinking or feeling. So there are four possible combinations, each producing a different set of characteristics—different interests, different values, different needs, different habits of mind and different surface traits.

Your own combination of perception and judgment makes a lot of difference in the kind of work you will do best and enjoy. If your daily work has most need for the kind of perception you naturally prefer, you will handle the job better and find it more satisfying. If your daily work has most need for the kind of deciding that comes naturally to you, your decisions will be better and will be made with more confidence. In choosing among careers, find out how much chance each will give you to use your own combination of perception and judgment.

EFFECTS OF THE COMBINATIONS OF
PERCEPTION AND JUDGMENT

Sensing plus Thinking. ST people are mainly interested in facts, since facts are what can be collected and verified directly by the senses—by seeing, hearing, touching, etc. And they make decisions on these facts by impersonal analysis, because the kind of judgment they trust is thinking, with its step-by-step process of reasoning from cause to effect, from premise to conclusion.

Sensing plus Feeling. SF people are also interested in facts, but make their decisions with personal warmth, because the kind of judgment they trust is feeling, with its power to weigh how much things matter to themselves and others.

Intuition plus Feeling. NF people make decisions with the same personal warmth. But, since they prefer intuition, their interest is not in facts but in possibilities, such as new projects, things that have not happened yet but might be made to happen, new truths that are not yet known but might be found out, or, above all, new possibilities for people.

Intuition plus Thinking. NT people share the interest in possibilities. But, since they prefer thinking, they approach these possibilities with impersonal analysis. Often the possibility they choose is a theoretical or technical one, with the human element more or less ignored.

The columns below present some of the results of these combinations.

	ST	SF	NF	NT
People who prefer:	SENSING + THINKING	SENSING + FEELING	INTUITION + FEELING	INTUITION + THINKING
focus their attention on:	Facts	Facts	Possibilities	Possibilities
and handle these with:	Impersonal analysis	Personal warmth	Personal warmth	Impersonal analysis
Thus they tend to become:	Practical and matter-of-fact	Sympathetic and friendly	Enthusiastic & insightful	Logical and ingenious
and find scope for their abilities in:	Technical skills with facts and objects	Practical help and services for people	Understanding & communicating with people	Theoretical and technical developments
for example:	Applied science Business Production Construction Etc.	Patient care Community service Sales Teaching Etc.	Behavioral science Research Literature & art Teaching Etc.	Physical science Research Management Forecasts & analysis Etc.

If you can tell which column comes closest to describing you, you can tell which two of the four processes (sensing, intuition, thinking and feeling) you naturally use most. One of those two will be your "favorite" process. The other is the "auxiliary" which supplies perception if the favorite is a judging process (T or F), or supplies judgment if the favorite is a perceptive process (S or N). Your greatest strengths come from the two you like, and it is important to trust and develop them. However, for some purposes, your less-liked kinds of perception and judgment will serve you much better—if you remember (and take the trouble) to use them.

MAKING FULL USE OF PERCEPTION AND JUDGMENT

To make full use of your perception and judgment, you need to use both kinds of perception and both kinds of judgment, each for the right purpose. This is a skill you can acquire by practice. Whenever you have a problem, a decision to make, a situation to deal with, try exercising each process by itself, consciously, purposefully, so that each can make its own contribution to the solution without interference from any other process. Start with your perceptive processes (S and N). Perception should always come before judgment.

1. Use your sensing for facing the facts, being realistic, finding exactly what the situation is, what you are doing, what other people are doing. Try to put aside all wishful thinking or sentiment that may blind you to the realities. Ask yourself how the situation would look to a wise, impartial bystander.

2. Use your intuition to discover all the possibilities—all the ways in which you might change the situation or your handling of it or other people's attitudes toward it. Try to put aside your natural assumption that you have been doing the one and only obviously right thing.

3. Use your thinking-judgment in an impersonal anal˙sis of cause and effect. Include all the consequences of the alternative solutions, pleasant and unpleasant, those that weigh against the solution you prefer as well as those in its favor. Try to count the full cost of everything. Examine every misgiving you may have been suppressing out of loyalty to someone or liking for something or reluctance to change your stand.

4. Use your feeling-judgment to weigh just how deeply you care about the things that will be gained or lost by each of the alternative solutions. Make a fresh appraisal, trying not to let the temporary outweigh the permanent, however agreeable or disagreeable the immediate prospect may be. Consider also how the other people concerned will feel about the various outcomes, even if you think it unreasonable of them. And include their feelings and your own feelings along with the other facts, in deciding which solution will work out best.

You will probably choose, as usual, a solution that appeals to your favorite process, but on a sounder basis than usual because you will have considered facts, possibilities, consequences and human values. Ignoring any of these can lead to trouble. Intuitives may base a decision on some possibility without discovering the facts that will make it impossible. Sensing types may settle for a faulty solution to a problem because they assume no better one is possible. Thinking types may ignore human values and feeling types may ignore consequences.

You will find some steps in this exercise easier than others. The ones that use your best processes are rather fun. The others are harder, but worthwhile. If feeling is your favorite process, the attempt to see all the consequences of an act may show you that even the best intentions can go wrong unless thought through. If thinking is your favorite process, the attempt to learn how others feel about your plans may show why you meet so much opposition.

What makes the hard steps hard is that they call for the strengths of types opposite to yours. When your problem is important, you may be wise to consult someone to whom these strengths come naturally. It is startling to see how different a given situation can look to a person of opposite type, but it will help you to understand and use the neglected opposite side of yourself.

MUTUAL USEFULNESS OF OPPOSITE TYPES

The clearest vision of the future comes only from an intuitive, the most practical realism only from a sensing type, the most incisive analysis only from a thinker, and the most skillful handling of people only from a feeling type. Success for any enterprise demands a variety of types, each in the right place.

Opposite types can supplement each other in any joint undertaking. When two people approach a problem from opposite sides, each sees things not visible to the other. Unfortunately, they seldom see each other's point of view. Too much oppositeness makes it hard for people to work well together. The best teamwork is usually done by people who differ on one or two preferences only. This much difference is useful, and the two or three preferences they have in common help them to understand each other and communicate.

When extreme opposites must work or live together, an understanding of type does much to lessen the friction. Disagreement is less irritating when Smith recognizes that it would hardly be normal for Jones to agree. Jones is not being willfully contrary. He is simply being an opposite type, and opposite types can be tremendously useful to each other when given the chance. The lists below show some of the specific ways.

INTUITIVES NEED SENSING TYPES:	SENSING TYPES NEED INTUITIVES:
To bring up pertinent facts	To bring up new possibilities
To apply experience to problems	To supply ingenuity on problems
To read the fine print in a contract	To read the signs of coming change
To notice what needs attention now	To see how to prepare for the future
To have patience	To have enthusiasm
To keep track of essential details	To watch for new essentials
To face difficulties with realism	To tackle difficulties with zest
To remind that the joys of the present are important	To show that the joys of the future are worth looking for

FEELING TYPES NEED THINKERS:	THINKERS NEED FEELING TYPES:
To analyze	To persuade
To organize	To conciliate
To find the flaws in advance	To forecast how others will feel
To reform what needs reforming	To arouse enthusiasm
To hold consistently to a policy	To teach
To weigh "the law and the evidence"	To sell
To fire people when necessary	To advertise
To stand firm against opposition	To appreciate the thinker

REMAINING PREFERENCES AND SUMMARY

Outer world or inner world: E or I. Your main fields of interest are apt to be directly related to the kind of perception and kind of judgment you prefer, that is, to your SN and TF preferences. But the sort of work you will most enjoy doing within those fields may depend on your EI preference,—whether you like to use your favorite process extravertedly (E) in the outer world of people and things, or introvertedly (I) in the inner world of concepts and ideas.

Take the ST people for example. The introverts among them (IST) like to organize facts and principles related to a situation, which is the useful thing to do in economics or law. The extraverts among them (EST) like to organize the situation itself (including any idle bystanders) and get it moving, which is the useful thing to do in business or industry.

Jung, who invented the terms, looked upon extraversion and introversion as valuable opposites, which everyone uses but not with equal ease. Extraverts tend to be more interested and comfortable when they are working actively with people or things. Introverts tend to be more interested and comfortable when their work involves ideas and requires a good deal of their activity to take place quietly inside their heads.

Judging attitude or perceptive attitude toward the outer world: J or P. The final preference, JP, is between the use of perception and the use of judgment in dealing with the outer world. The J people rely mainly on a judging process for this purpose (thinking or feeling, whichever they prefer), and live in a planned, decided, orderly way, wanting to regulate life and control it. The P people rely mainly on a perceptive process (sensing or intuition) for dealing with the outer world, and live in a flexible, spontaneous way, wanting to understand life and adapt to it.

This JP preference works differently with extraverts and introverts. With extraverts the favorite process is, by definition, the one they prefer to use in the outer world. Therefore the extraverts' favorite process governs their JP preference. Extraverts whose favorite process is a judging one come out J. Extraverts whose favorite process is a perceptive one come out P.

With introverts the favorite process is, by definition, the one they prefer to use in the inner world. They do their extraverting mostly with their auxiliary. Their auxiliary process, therefore, is what governs their JP preference. Introverts whose favorite process is a judging one come out P because their auxiliary is perceptive. And introverts whose favorite process is a perceptive one come out J.

Summary of the four preferences.
Your type is the result of your own combination of preferences, which can be stated for convenience in four letters. For example, ISTJ means an introvert liking sensing and thinking and a mainly judging attitude toward the outer world. ENFP means an extravert liking intuition and feeling and a mainly perceptive attitude toward the outer world. (N is used for intuition because I stands for introversion.) The Type Table on the back cover shows the favorite and auxiliary processes for each of the sixteen types. Brief sketches are given on pp. 7-8, longer descriptions on pp. 9-16.

EI Preference
Extraversion   Introversion

SN Preference
Sensing   Intuition

TF Preference
Thinking   Feeling

JP Preference
Judgment   Perception

EFFECTS OF THE COMBINATIONS OF ALL

		SENSING TYPES WITH THINKING	SENSING TYPES WITH FEELING
INTROVERTS	JUDGING	**ISTJ** Serious, quiet, earn success by concentration and thoroughness. Practical, orderly, matter-of-fact, logical, realistic and dependable. See to it that everything is well organized. Take responsibility. Make up their own minds as to what should be accomplished and work toward it steadily, regardless of protests or distractions. Live their outer life more with thinking, inner more with sensing.	**ISFJ** Quiet, friendly, responsible and conscientious. Work devotedly to meet their obligations and serve their friends and school. Thorough, painstaking, accurate. May need time to master technical subjects, as their interests are not often technical. Patient with detail and routine. Loyal, considerate, concerned with how other people feel. Live their outer life more with feeling, inner more with sensing.
INTROVERTS	PERCEPTIVE	**ISTP** Cool onlookers, quiet, reserved, observing and analyzing life with detached curiosity and unexpected flashes of original humor. Usually interested in impersonal principles, cause and effect, or how and why mechanical things work. Exert themselves no more than they think necessary, because any waste of energy would be inefficient. Live their outer life more with sensing, inner more with thinking.	**ISFP** Retiring, quietly friendly, sensitive, modest about their abilities. Shun disagreements, do not force their opinions or values on others. Usually do not care to lead but are often loyal followers. May be rather relaxed about assignments or getting things done, because they enjoy the present moment and do not want to spoil it by undue haste or exertion. Live their outer life more with sensing, inner more with feeling.
EXTRAVERTS	PERCEPTIVE	**ESTP** Matter-of-fact, do not worry or hurry, enjoy whatever comes along. Tend to like mechanical things and sports, with friends on the side. May be a bit blunt or insensitive. Can do math or science when they see the need. Dislike long explanations. Are best with real things that can be worked, handled, taken apart or put back together. Live their outer life more with sensing, inner more with thinking.	**ESFP** Outgoing, easygoing, accepting, friendly, fond of a good time. Like sports and making things. Know what's going on and join in eagerly. Find remembering facts easier than mastering theories. Are best in situations that need sound common sense and practical ability with people as well as with things. Live their outer life more with sensing, inner more with feeling.
EXTRAVERTS	JUDGING	**ESTJ** Practical realists, matter-of-fact, with a natural head for business or mechanics. Not interested in subjects they see no use for, but can apply themselves when necessary. Like to organize and run activities. Tend to run things well, especially if they remember to consider other people's feelings and points of view when making their decisions. Live their outer life more with thinking, inner more with sensing.	**ESFJ** Warm-hearted, talkative, popular, conscientious, born cooperators, active committee members. Always doing something nice for someone. Work best with plenty of encouragement and praise. Little interest in abstract thinking or technical subjects. Main interest is in things that directly and visibly affect people's lives. Live their outer life more with feeling, inner more with sensing.

FOUR PREFERENCES IN YOUNG PEOPLE

INTUITIVES

WITH FEELING	WITH THINKING
INFJ Succeed by perseverance, originality and desire to do whatever is needed or wanted. Put their best efforts into their work. Quietly forceful, conscientious, concerned for others. Respected for their firm principles. Likely to be honored and followed for their clear convictions as to how best to serve the common good. Live their outer life more with feeling, inner more with intuition.	**INTJ** Have original minds and great drive which they use only for their own purposes. In fields that appeal to them they have a fine power to organize a job and carry it through with or without help. Skeptical, critical, independent, determined, often stubborn. Must learn to yield less important points in order to win the most important. Live their outer life more with thinking, inner more with intuition.
INFP Full of enthusiasms and loyalties, but seldom talk of these until they know you well. Care about learning, ideas, language, and independent projects of their own. Apt to be on yearbook staff, perhaps as editor. Tend to undertake too much, then somehow get it done. Friendly, but often too absorbed in what they are doing to be sociable or notice much. Live their outer life more with intuition, inner more with feeling.	**INTP** Quiet, reserved, brilliant in exams, especially in theoretical or scientific subjects. Logical to the point of hair-splitting. Interested mainly in ideas, with little liking for parties or small talk. Tend to have very sharply defined interests. Need to choose careers where some strong interest of theirs can be used and useful. Live their outer life more with intuition, inner more with thinking.
ENFP Warmly enthusiastic, high-spirited, ingenious, imaginative. Able to do almost anything that interests them. Quick with a solution for any difficulty and ready to help anyone with a problem. Often rely on their ability to improvise instead of preparing in advance. Can always find compelling reasons for whatever they want. Live their outer life more with intuition, inner more with feeling.	**ENTP** Quick, ingenious, good at many things. Stimulating company, alert and outspoken, argue for fun on either side of a question. Resourceful in solving new and challenging problems, but may neglect routine assignments. Turn to one new interest after another. Can always find logical reasons for whatever they want. Live their outer life more with intuition, inner more with thinking.
ENFJ Responsive and responsible. Feel real concern for what others think and want, and try to handle things with due regard for other people's feelings. Can present a proposal or lead a group discussion with ease and tact. Sociable, popular, active in school affairs, but put time enough on their studies to do good work. Live their outer life more with feeling, inner more with intuition.	**ENTJ** Hearty, frank, able in studies, leaders in activities. Usually good in anything that requires reasoning and intelligent talk, such as public speaking. Are well-informed and keep adding to their fund of knowledge. May sometimes be more positive and confident than their experience in an area warrants. Live their outer life more with thinking, inner more with intuition.

INTROVERTS
JUDGING PERCEPTIVE

PERCEPTIVE JUDGING
EXTRAVERTS

A-8

EXTRAVERTED THINKING TYPES
ESTJ and ENTJ

Extraverted thinkers use their thinking to run as much of the world as may be theirs to run. They organize their facts and operations well in advance, define their objectives and make a systematic drive to reach these objectives on schedule. Through reliance on thinking, they become logical, analytical, often critical, impersonal and unlikely to be convinced by anything but reasoning.

They enjoy being executives, deciding what ought to be done, and giving the necessary orders. They have little patience with confusion, inefficiency, halfway measures, or anything aimless and ineffective, and they know how to be tough when the situation calls for toughness.

They think conduct should be governed by logic, and govern their own that way as much as they can. They live according to a definite formula that embodies their basic judgments about the world. Any change in their ways requires a deliberate change in the formula.

Like other judging types, they run some risk of neglecting perception. They need to stop and listen to the other person's side of the matter, especially with people who are not in a position to talk back. They seldom find this easy, but if (repeat, _if_) they do not manage to do it, they may judge too hastily, without enough facts or enough regard for what other people think or feel.

Feeling is their least developed process. If they suppress or neglect it too long, it can explode in damaging ways. They need to make some conscious use of feeling, preferably in appreciation of other people's merits,—an art that comes less naturally to thinkers than to feeling types. Thinkers can, if they will, "make it a rule" in their formula to mention what is well done, not merely what needs correcting. The results will be worthwhile, both in their work and in their private lives.

ESTJ
With sensing as auxiliary

Look at things with their sensing rather than their intuition. Hence are most interested in realities perceived by their five senses, which makes them matter-of-fact, practical, realistic, factually-minded, concerned with here and now. More curious about new things than new ideas. Want ideas, plans and decisions to be based on solid fact.

Solve problems by expertly applying and adapting past experience.

Like work where they can achieve immediate, visible and tangible results. Have a natural bent for business and industry, production and construction. Enjoy administration and getting things organized and done. Do not listen to their own intuition very much, so tend to need an intuitive around to sell them on the value of new ideas.

ENTJ
With intuition as auxiliary

Look at things with their intuition rather than their sensing, hence are mainly interested in seeing the possibilities beyond what is present or obvious or known. Intuition heightens their intellectual interest, curiosity for new ideas, tolerance for theory, taste for complex problems, insight, vision and concern for long range consequences.

Are seldom content in jobs that make no demand on intuition. Need problems to solve and are expert at finding new solutions. Interest is in the broad picture, not in detailed procedures or facts. Tend to choose like-minded intuitives as associates. Also tend to need someone with sensing around to keep them from overlooking relevant facts and important details.

INTROVERTED THINKING TYPES
ISTP and INTP

Introverted thinkers use their thinking to analyze the world, not to run it. They organize ideas and facts, not situations or people unless they must. Relying on thinking makes them logical, impersonal, objectively critical, not likely to be convinced by anything but reasoning. Being introverts, they focus their thinking on the principles underlying things rather than on the things themselves. Since it is hard to switch their thinking from ideas to details of daily living, they lead their outer lives mainly with their preferred perceptive process, S or N. They are quiet, reserved, detachedly curious and quite adaptable—till one of their ruling principles is violated, at which point they stop adapting.

If (repeat, _if_) they do not develop their perception, they will have too little knowledge or experience of the world. Their thinking will have no real relationship to the problems of their time, and not very much will come of it.

In the field of ideas they are decisive, though socially they may be rather shy except with their best friends. Their special problem is to make their ideas understood. Wanting to state exact truth, they tend to state it in a way too complicated for most people to follow. If they will use simple statements, even if they think the point is too obvious to be worth making, their ideas will be much more widely understood and accepted.

Feeling is their least developed process. They are not apt to know, unless told, what matters emotionally to another person. They should recognize that most people do care about having their merits appreciated and their point of view respectfully considered. And they should act accordingly. Both their working life and personal life will go better if they take the trouble to do two simple things—say an appreciative word when praise is honestly due, and mention the points where they agree with another person _before_ they bring up the points where they disagree.

ISTP	INTP
With sensing as auxiliary	With intuition as auxiliary

See the realities. Great capacity for facts and details. Good at applied science and at mechanics and the properties of materials and things. With nontechnical interests, can use general principles to bring order out of masses of confused data and meaning out of unorganized facts. May be analysts of markets, sales, securities or statistics of any kind.

Likely to be patient, accurate, good with their hands, fond of sports and outdoors, and have a gift of fun.

Great believers in economy of effort, which is an asset if they judge accurately how much effort is needed, and do efficiently what the situation demands. If not, economy of effort can become mere laziness and little will get done.

See the possibilities. Value facts mainly in relation to theory. Good at pure science, research, math, and the more complicated engineering problems. With nontechnical interests, make scholars, teachers, abstract thinkers in economics, philosophy, psychology, etc.

Apt to have insight, ingenuity, quick understanding, intellectual curiosity, fertility of ideas about problems. More interested in reaching solutions than in putting them into practice, which others can do as well.

Need to check out even their most attractive intuitive projects against the facts and the limitations these impose. Otherwise may squander their energies in pursuing impossibilities.

EXTRAVERTED FEELING TYPES
ESFJ and ENFJ

Extraverted feeling types radiate warmth and fellowship. Reliance on feeling gives them a very personal approach to life, since feeling judges everything by a set of personal values. Being extraverts, they focus their feeling on the people around them, placing a very high value on harmonious human contacts. They are friendly, tactful, sympathetic, and can almost always express the right feeling.

They are particularly warmed by approval and sensitive to indifference. Much of their pleasure and satisfaction comes not only from others' warmth of feeling but from their own; they enjoy admiring people and so tend to concentrate on a person's most admirable qualities. They try to live up to their ideals and are loyal to respected persons, institutions and causes.

They are unusually able to see value in other people's opinions. And even when the opinions are conflicting, they have faith that harmony can somehow be achieved and often manage to bring it about. Their intense concentration on other people's viewpoints sometimes makes them lose sight of the value of their own. They are best at jobs that deal with people and any situation where the needed cooperation can be won by good will. They think best when talking with people and enjoy talk. It takes special effort for them to be brief and businesslike.

Being judging types, they like to have matters settled and decided, but they do not need or want to make all the decisions themselves. They have many "shoulds" and "should nots" and may express these freely. They are conscientious, persevering, orderly even in small matters, and inclined to expect others to be the same.

If (repeat if) they do not develop their perception, they will, with the best of intentions, act on assumptions that turn out to be wrong. They are especially likely to be blind to the facts when there is a situation that is disagreeable or a criticism that hurts. It is harder for them than for other types to see things they wish were not true. If they fail to face disagreeable facts, they will sweep their problems under the rug instead of finding good solutions.

ESFJ
With sensing as auxiliary

Look at things with their sensing, which makes them practical, realistic, matter-of-fact, concerned with here and now. Appreciate and enjoy their material possessions and details of direct experience. Like to base plans and decisions upon known facts.

Enjoy variety, but usually adapt excellently to routine.

Compassion and awareness of physical conditions often attract them to nursing (where they provide warmth and comfort as well as devoted care) and to health professions in general.

ENFJ
With intuition as auxiliary

Look at things with their intuition rather than their sensing, hence are mainly interested in seeing the possibilities beyond what is present or obvious or known. Intuition heightens their understanding, long-range vision, insight, curiosity about new ideas, love of books and tolerance for theory.

Likely to have a gift of expression, but may use it in speaking to audiences rather than in writing. Interest in possibilities for people attracts them often to counseling in the fields of career choice or personal development.

INTROVERTED FEELING TYPES
ISFP and INFP

Introverted feeling types have a wealth of warmth and enthusiasm, but may not show it till they know you well. Reliance on feeling leads them to judge everything by personal values; being introverts, they choose these values without reference to the judgment of others. They know what is most important to them and protect it at all costs. Loyalties and ideals govern their lives. Their deepest feelings are seldom expressed, since their tenderness and passionate conviction are masked by their quiet reserve.

Their feeling being introverted, they conduct their outer lives mainly with their preferred perceptive process, either sensing or intuition. This makes them open-minded, flexible and adaptable—until one of the things they value most deeply seems in danger—at which point they stop adapting. Except for the sake of their work they have little wish to impress or dominate. The friends who mean most to them are the people who understand their values and the goals they are working toward.

They are twice as good when working at a job they believe in; their feeling puts added energy behind their efforts. They want their work to contribute to something that matters to them—human understanding or happiness or health, or perhaps to the perfecting of some project or undertaking. They want to have a purpose beyond their paycheck, no matter how big the check. They are perfectionists wherever their feeling is engaged and are usually happiest at some individual work involving their personal values.

Being idealists, they measure their accomplishments against an inner standard of perfection, instead of what is actually possible. They may suffer from too great self-demand, feeling that the contrast between their inner ideal and outer reality is somehow their fault. They need to find something they really care about, and then work to achieve it. With an ideal to work for, and good development of perception to help them recognize realistic difficulties and possible solutions, they can achieve a high degree of self-confident drive.

If (repeat if) they do not find a way to use their energies in the service of an ideal, they tend to become oversensitive and vulnerable, losing confidence in life and in themselves. If their perception is undeveloped, they may have so little realism that they aspire to the impossible and achieve frustratingly little.

ISFP With sensing as auxiliary	INFP With intuition as auxiliary
See the realities. Mildly resemble ESFP, especially in seeing and meeting the need of the moment. Can pay close, unbroken attention for long periods, when work requires monitoring or close observation. Show their warmth more by deeds than words. Compassionate toward all helpless creatures. Work well at jobs requiring devotion. Gentle, considerate, retiring. Consistently underestimate and understate themselves. May find satisfactory outlets in fields where taste, discrimination and a sense of beauty are of value.	See the possibilities. Mildly resemble ENFP, especially in liking to concentrate on projects and disliking details not related to a deep interest. Understanding, tend to have insight and long-range vision. Curious about new ideas, fond of books and language. Apt to have skill in expressing themselves. Ingenious and persuasive on the subject of their enthusiasms. Especially interested in possibilities for people. Enjoy counseling and teaching. With high ability, may excel in literature, art, science or psychology.

EXTRAVERTED SENSING TYPES

ESTP and ESFP

Extraverted sensing makes the adaptable realists, who good-naturedly accept and use the facts around them, whatever these are. They know what the facts are, since they notice and remember more than any other type. They know what goes on, who wants what and who doesn't. And they do not fight those facts. There is a sort of effortless economy in the way they deal with a situation, never taking the hard way when an easier one will work.

Often they can get other people to adapt, too. Being perceptive types, they look for the satisfying solution, instead of trying to impose any "should" or "must" of their own, and people generally like them well enough to consider any compromise that they suggest "might work". They are unprejudiced, open-minded, and usually patient, easygoing and tolerant of everyone—including themselves. They enjoy life. They don't get wrought up. Thus they may be very good at easing tense situations and pulling conflicting factions together.

Their expert sensing may show itself: (a) in a gift for machinery and the handling of tools and materials for craft or artistic purposes, or in ability to recognize quality, line, color, texture or detail; (b) in a capacity for exact facts, even when separate and unrelated, and the ability to absorb, remember and apply them; (c) in a continuous awareness, an ability to see the need of the moment and turn easily to meet it.

They are strong in the art of living, appreciate and enjoy their material possessions, and take the time to acquire and care for these. They value enjoyment, from good food and good clothes to music, art and all the products of the amusement industry. Even without these helps, they get fun out of life, which makes them fun to be with.

Being realists, they get more from first-hand experience than from study, are more effective on the job than on written tests, and doubly effective when on familiar ground. Seeing the value of new ideas, theories and possibilities may well come a bit hard, because intuition is their least developed process.

Their net effectiveness depends on whether they develop their judgment to the point where it can balance their easygoing sensing and give some direction to their lives. If (repeat, if) their judgment is not good enough to give them any character or stick-to-it-iveness, they may adapt mainly to their own love of a good time, and become lazy, unstable and generally shallow.

ESTP With thinking as auxiliary	ESFP With feeling as auxiliary
Like to make decisions with their thinking rather than their feeling. Hence are more aware of the logical consequences of an act or decision. Thinking gives them more grasp of underlying principles, helps with math and theory and makes it easier for them to get tough when the situation calls for toughness.	Like to make decisions with their feeling rather than their thinking. Feeling gives them tact, sympathy, interest in people, ease in handling human contacts, and may make them too easy as disciplinarians. Feeling also makes for artistic taste and judgment, but is no help with analysis.

INTROVERTED SENSING TYPES

ISTJ and ISFJ

Introverted sensing types are made particularly dependable by their combination of preferences. They use their favorite process, sensing, in their inner life, and base their ideas on a deep, solid accumulation of stored impressions, which gives them some pretty unshakable ideas. Then they use their preferred kind of judgment, thinking or feeling, to run their outer life. Thus they have a complete, realistic, practical respect both for the facts and for whatever responsibilities these facts create. Sensing provides the facts. And after the introvert's characteristic pause for reflection, their judgment accepts the responsibilities.

They can remember and use any number of facts, but want them all accurate. They like everything kept factual, clearly stated, not too complex. Not till you know them very well do you discover that behind their outer calm they are seeing the facts from an intensely individual, often delightfully humorous angle. Their private reaction, the way a thing will strike them, is quite unpredictable.

But what they actually do about it will be sound and sensible because what they do is part of their outer life and so is governed by their best judgment. No type is more thorough, painstaking, systematic, hard-working, or patient with detail and routine. Their perseverance tends to stabilize everything with which they are connected. They do not enter into things impulsively, but once in, they are very hard to distract, discourage or stop. They do not quit unless experience convinces them they are wrong.

As administrators, their practical judgment and memory for detail make them conservative, consistent, able to cite cases to support their evaluations of people and methods. They will go to any amount of trouble if they "can see the need of it," but hate to be required to do anything that "doesn't make sense." Usually it is hard for them to see any sense in needs that differ widely from their own. But once they are convinced that a given thing does matter a lot to a given person, the need becomes a fact to be respected and they may go to generous lengths to help satisfy it, while still holding that it doesn't make sense.

Their effectiveness depends on their developing adequate judgment for dealing with the world. If (repeat, if) judgment remains childish, the world is not dealt with, the person retreats into silent preoccupation with inner reactions to sense-impressions, and not much of value is likely to result.

ISTJ With thinking as auxiliary	ISFJ With feeling as auxiliary
Mildly resemble the extraverted thinking types.	Mildly resemble the extraverted feeling types.
Thinking stresses analysis, logic and decisiveness.	Feeling stresses loyalty, consideration and the common welfare.
In their personal relationships, they may need to take extra pains to understand and appreciate. They will then be in no danger of overriding people less forceful than they are, and will find themselves richly repaid both in their work and in their private lives.	They are sympathetic, tactful, kind and genuinely concerned, which traits make them very supportive to persons in need of support. They are often attracted to fields where systematic attention to detail is combined with a care for people, as in the health professions.

EXTRAVERTED INTUITIVE TYPES

ENTP and ENFP

The extraverted intuitives are the enthusiastic innovators. They are always seeing new possibilities—new ways of doing things, or quite new and fascinating things that might be done—and they go all out in pursuit of these. They have a lot of imagination and initiative for originating projects, and a lot of impulsive energy for carrying them out. They are wholly confident of the worth of their inspirations, tireless with the problems involved, and ingenious with the difficulties. They get so interested in the current project that they think of little else.

They get other people interested too. Being perceptive types, they try to understand people rather than to judge them; often, by putting their minds to it, they achieve an uncanny knowledge of what makes a given person tick, and use this to win support for their project. They adapt to other people in the way they present their objective, but never to the point of giving it up. Their faith in their intuition makes them too independent and individualistic to be conformists, but they keep a lively circle of contacts as a consequence of their versatility and their easy interest in almost everything.

In their quieter moments, their auxiliary gives them some balancing introversion and adds depth to the insights supplied by their intuition. At its best, their insight, tempered by judgment, may amount to wisdom.

Their trouble is that they hate uninspired routine and find it remarkably hard to apply themselves to humdrum detail unconnected with any major interest. Worse yet, even their projects begin to seem routine and lose attraction as soon as the main problems are solved and the rest seems clear sailing. They may discipline themselves to carry through, but they are happiest and most effective in jobs that permit of one project after another, with someone else taking over as soon as the situation is well in hand.

If their judgment and self-discipline are not developed, they will throw themselves into ill-chosen projects, leave them unfinished, and squander their inspirations, abilities and energies on unimportant, half-done jobs. At their worst, they will be unstable, undependable, fickle and easily discouraged.

ENTP
With thinking as auxiliary

More independent, analytical and critical of their inspirations, more impersonal in their relations with people, more apt to consider only how others may affect their projects and not how the projects may affect others.

May be inventors, scientists, troubleshooters, promoters, or almost anything that it interests them to be.

ENFP
With feeling as auxiliary

More enthusiastic, more concerned with people and skillful in handling them. Much drawn to counseling, where each new person presents a fresh problem to be solved and fresh possibilities to be communicated.

May be inspired and inspiring teachers, scientists, artists, advertising or sales people, or almost anything that it interests them to be.

INTROVERTED INTUITIVE TYPES

INTJ and INFJ

The introverted intuitives are the great innovators in the field of ideas. They trust their intuitive insights as to the relationships and meanings of things, regardless of established authority or popular beliefs. They trust their vision of the possibilities, regardless of universal skepticism. And they want to see their ideas worked out in practice, accepted and applied.

Consequently, they have to deal firmly with the outer world, which they do by means of their preferred kind of judgment, either T or F. Thus they back up their original insight with the determination, perseverance and enduring purpose of the judging types. When they are driving to turn an inspiration into a reality, problems stimulate rather than discourage them. The impossible takes a little longer—but not much.

Certain dangers arise from their single-minded concentration. They see their goal so clearly that they may not even look for the other things they need to see—the things that conflict with their goal. They may not take the trouble to learn the details of the situation they propose to change. Since sensing is their least developed process, they can easily overlook relevant facts and the limitations these facts impose.

They may not consider the opposition they will meet, its strength or source or probable grounds. They may not consider the possibility that something is wrong with their idea. In scientific research or engineering design, a trial of their boldly ingenious ideas will visibly succeed—or fail and show where the idea <u>has</u> to be revised. They need to be particularly alert for flaws in their ideas in those fields where their insights cannot be tested so clearly.

Their auxiliary process, if adequately developed, can supply needed criticism of their ideas. Judgment can be used to foresee difficulties and decide what needs to be done about them. Most original inspirations need to be modified in the light of facts. Ideas need to be worked out and perfected to lessen objections. The best ideas still need to be presented to the world in terms understandable to other types.

If (repeat, <u>if</u>) their judgment is <u>not</u> developed, they cannot criticize their own inner vision, and they tend to reject all judgments from outside. As a result, they cannot shape their inspirations into effective action. Their ideas will go to waste, and they may be regarded only as visionaries or cranks.

INTJ With thinking as auxiliary	INFJ With feeling as auxiliary
Most individualistic and most independent of all the types. Resemble extraverted thinkers in organizing ability and a tendency to ignore the views and feelings of those who don't agree with them. Logical, critical, decisive, determined, often stubborn. Tend to drive others almost as hard as they drive themselves. Apt to be effective, relentless reorganizers. Can be efficient executives, rich in ideas.	Less obviously individualistic, more apt to win cooperation than to demand it. Resemble extraverted feeling types in their sympathetic handling of people and in a tendency to ignore harsh and uncongenial facts. May apply their ingenuity to problems of human welfare on their own and in their own way. Can be successful executives, especially where affairs can be conducted on a personal basis.

EFFECTS OF EACH PREFERENCE IN WORK SITUATIONS

EXTRAVERTS	INTROVERTS
Like variety and action.	Like quiet for concentration.
Tend to be faster, dislike complicated procedures.	Tend to be careful with details, dislike sweeping statements.
Are often good at greeting people.	Have trouble remembering names and faces.
Are often impatient with long slow jobs.	Tend not to mind working on one project for a long time uninterruptedly.
Are interested in the results of their job, in getting it done and in how other people do it.	Are interested in the idea behind their job.
Often do not mind the interruption of answering the telephone.	Dislike telephone intrusions and interruptions.
Often act quickly, sometimes without thinking.	Like to think a lot before they act, sometimes without acting.
Like to have people around.	Work contentedly alone.
Usually communicate freely.	Have some problems communicating.

THINKING TYPES	FEELING TYPES
Do not show emotion readily and are often uncomfortable dealing with people's feelings.	Tend to be very aware of other people and their feelings.
May hurt people's feelings without knowing it.	Enjoy pleasing people, even in unimportant things.
Like analysis and putting things into logical order. Can get along without harmony.	Like harmony. Efficiency may be badly disturbed by office feuds.
Tend to decide impersonally, sometimes paying insufficient attention to people's wishes.	Often let decisions be influenced by their own or other people's personal likes and wishes.
Need to be treated fairly.	Need occasional praise.
Are able to reprimand people or fire them when necessary.	Dislike telling people unpleasant things.
Are more analytically oriented—respond more easily to people's thoughts.	Are more people-oriented—respond more easily to people's values.
Tend to be firm-minded.	Tend to be sympathetic.

EFFECTS OF EACH PREFERENCE IN WORK SITUATIONS

SENSING TYPES

Dislike new problems unless there are standard ways to solve them.

Like an established way of doing things.

Enjoy using skills already learned more than learning new ones.

Work more steadily, with realistic idea of how long it will take.

Usually reach a conclusion step by step.

Are patient with routine details.

Are impatient when the details get complicated.

Are not often inspired, and rarely trust the inspiration when they are.

Seldom make errors of fact.

Tend to be good at precise work.

INTUITIVE TYPES

Like solving new problems.

Dislike doing the same thing repeatedly.

Enjoy learning a new skill more than using it.

Work in bursts of energy powered by enthusiasm, with slack periods in between.

Reach a conclusion quickly.

Are impatient with routine details.

Are patient with complicated situations.

Follow their inspirations, good or bad.

Frequently make errors of fact.

Dislike taking time for precision.

JUDGING TYPES

Work best when they can plan their work and follow the plan.

Like to get things settled and finished.

May decide things too quickly.

May dislike to interrupt the project they are on for a more urgent one.

May not notice new things that need to be done.

Want only the essentials needed to begin their work.

Tend to be satisfied once they reach a judgment on a thing, situation, or person.

PERCEPTIVE TYPES

Adapt well to changing situations.

Do not mind leaving things open for alterations.

May have trouble making decisions.

May start too many projects and have difficulty in finishing them.

May postpone unpleasant jobs.

Want to know all about a new job.

Tend to be curious and welcome new light on a thing, situation, or person.

TYPE TABLE

		EXTRAVERTS	
JUDGING	PERCEPTIVE	PERCEPTIVE	JUDGING

INTUITIVES

WITH THINKING

ISTJ Introverted Sensing with thinking	ISFJ Introverted Sensing with feeling	INFJ Introverted Intuition with feeling	INTJ Introverted Intuition with thinking

| ISTP Introverted Thinking with sensing | ISFP Introverted Feeling with sensing | INFP Introverted Feeling with intuition | INTP Introverted Thinking with intuition |

| ESTP Extraverted Sensing with thinking | ESFP Extraverted Sensing with feeling | ENFP Extraverted Intuition with feeling | ENTP Extraverted Intuition with thinking |

| ESTJ Extraverted Thinking with sensing | ESFJ Extraverted Feeling with sensing | ENFJ Extraverted Feeling with intuition | ENTJ Extraverted Thinking with intuition |

INTJ — Introverted Intuition with thinking
INTP — Introverted Thinking with intuition
ENTP — Extraverted Intuition with thinking
ENTJ — Extraverted Thinking with intuition
INFJ — Introverted Intuition with feeling
INFP — Introverted Feeling with intuition
ENFP — Extraverted Intuition with feeling
ENFJ — Extraverted Feeling with intuition
ISFJ — Introverted Sensing with feeling
ISFP — Introverted Feeling with sensing
ESFP — Extraverted Sensing with feeling
ESFJ — Extraverted Feeling with sensing
ISTJ — Introverted Sensing with thinking
ISTP — Introverted Thinking with sensing
ESTP — Extraverted Sensing with thinking
ESTJ — Extraverted Thinking with sensing